# ENGAGEMENT FUNDRAISING

How to raise more money for less in the 21st century

# ENGAGEMENT FUNDRAISING

How to raise more money for less in the 21$^{st}$ century

**Greg Warner**

Engagement Fundraising
Copyright @2018 by Greg Warner

Published by MarketSmart

Hardcover ISBN: 978-1-7322628-0-5
Trade Paperback ISBN: 978-1-7322628-1-2
eISBN: 978-1-7322628-2-9

# Inscription

This is for the donors, volunteers, advocates, and members who want to change the world but need an organization bigger than them to get it done.

This is for the employees at nonprofits who work tirelessly for the donors, volunteers, advocates, and members.

And most of all, this is for the people who desperately depend on all of the above. People like my wife, Nessa, whom I love more than anything in the world. She needs a cure for her type 1 diabetes—the wretched disease that has encumbered her life since she was just nine years old.

This is for others like her: the sick, the poor, and the hungry. The wounded, underserved, and distressed. The defenseless, needy, and unfortunate.

This is for humanity and for generations to come.

# Table of Contents

Introduction
# Who Is This Guy?

I never intended to write this book.

In fact, I never thought I'd write any book at all. I also never anticipated I would be involved in fundraising. It wasn't in my original life plan.

As long as I can remember, I wanted to have my own ad agency. When I was a kid, I doodled new logos for 80s rock bands on the brown paper bags that covered my schoolbooks. I painted album covers on the backs of my friends' denim jackets. I even created a bunch of posters for a friend running a campaign to be on the student council.

I was voted "Class Artist" in my high school yearbook, but I always believed I was more than an artist. I thought of myself as a promoter, a publicist, a marketer. I was always fascinated with promotions and found power in words and emotion in images. *How can one person motivate the masses with a single headline, logo, or picture?* I'd wonder.

When I visited my dad's little townhouse every other weekend in Princeton, New Jersey, I would sometimes talk to his next-door neighbor, Barton Cummings. He was a nice old man who liked to talk to me about his days in the advertising business.

It was serendipitous because he happened to be the former CEO of Compton Advertising, one of the largest advertising firms in the country that he built to become an international agency. It was later purchased by Saatchi & Saatchi, a firm that now has a network of 140 offices in 76 countries with over 6,500 employees.

Bart was known as a "benevolent dictator" because he was responsible for building the great product brands of the 1950s that changed consumer preferences and altered buyer purchase behaviors. His most famous clients were Proctor & Gamble, U.S. Steel, and the New York Stock Exchange.

His was the golden age of advertising—the days when admen drank stiff martinis and dined with their clients to get the opportunity to spend their budgets and sear the images of their brands into the minds of consumers everywhere. I wanted to be one of those guys.

Before I finally opened my own marketing shop, I worked for one magazine, two newspapers, two ad agencies, a direct marketing firm, and a printer. Finally, in 2008, I launched MarketSmart inside a filthy, run-down warehouse. Starting a business during the Great Recession was either crazy or stupid—or both.

We were daring. We would take risks. We wouldn't shy away from challenges.

Our niche was generating highly qualified leads for sales teams in the private sector. We got excited when our efforts drew forth responses so salespeople could close bigger deals faster and more cost-effectively.

Results were the oxygen we breathed.

We grew. But as our revenues increased, the business became less fulfilling for me. After a while, it seemed like everything I ever wanted wasn't everything I really needed.

My heart yearned for something more meaningful. I began to ask myself, "How can I add more significance to my life?" The answer came in my mailbox.

# The Letter That Changed My Life

A diabetes charity sent me a newsletter. We were regular donors, so getting yet another piece of mail from them was nothing new. Yet, that particular newsletter changed my life forever.

It was filled with legal jargon. It was confusing. Although most people receiving this newsletter would have thrown it away immediately, I took a good, hard look. As a marketer, I was curious. I wanted to figure out what they wanted me to do.

After some thoughtful examination and consideration, I realized they wanted me to give their organization a legacy gift that would be realized after my lifetime. The method they recommended was a charitable gift annuity, a strategic giving option set aside mostly for people over the age of 65. I was 37.

It wasn't the first time I considered the wasteful nature of charity marketing. My beloved Uncle Sid died from melanoma several years before I received that newsletter. Soon after his death, my cousins started a nonprofit foundation to raise money. Every year, our entire family and a bunch of friends worked tirelessly on a fundraising golf tournament and banquet. Its mission was to educate the public about the dangers of the sun and how to protect oneself from skin cancer.

Sounds nice, right? It *was* nice. But nice wasn't the point.

I would go to the event every year, but privately I thought there had to be a better way. I saw how inefficient and ineffective our actions were. After all of the costs and expenses, very little money was left for the charity. The foundation made the family and community feel good for a while, but we really weren't making a big enough impact. Eventually, everyone got tired and lost interest, and the endeavor was laid to rest.

# The Path to Creating Change

The experience with the diabetes charity's newsletter ticked me off. As time passed, a lot of what I learned about nonprofits left me irritated. As a donor, I often found myself feeling angry and annoyed. Over time, telemarketing calls interrupted my meals and direct mailers filled my trash cans. The more I examined nonprofits' marketing efforts, the more incensed I became.

Eventually, I found myself reading balance sheets and 990s to unravel how some nonprofits expertly shift numbers around to make it seem as though the donations they receive efficiently support their missions—not their expenses. For instance, a clever CFO can ensure that events such as bike rides or 5k races magically become educational events, not fundraisers. The trick is simple: just lay out some informational brochures nearby.

I don't blame them for playing those games. Donors have been trained by the media and others to frown upon nonprofits' spending of money to raise money. Yet blaming the media isn't the answer either.

In many cases, the media's scrutiny of evildoers has been warranted. In August of 2012, the *Los Angeles Times* reported on its investigations into the Boy Scouts of America during which it allegedly found cover-ups of sexual abuse and improper screening of trusted volunteers. This seemingly led to more stringent background checks on potential volunteers and a policy of reporting suspicions of abuse to police.

In September of the same year, two large for-profit fundraising service providers were forced to defend their practices. *Bloomberg Markets* magazine reported on the telemarketing firm InfoCision Management, finding practices that included examples of telemarketers lying to donors, while (in one case) only 22 percent of donation revenues went to the charities for which they were intended.

In the same year, CNN reported on another service provider, Quadriga Art, alleging that the Disabled Veterans National Foundation paid the firm more than it had received in donations (at least on paper). Something screwy was going on but the firm's public relations team argued that the coverage was unbalanced and showed a misunderstanding of both the industry and what their client does.

Stories like these scared donors, leading them to lump the bad apples with the good and driving them to turn to charity vetting sites such as Charity Navigator and GuideStar. Too often, donors use those sites to focus solely on what percent of their donations go to the cause compared with the amount supporting administrative expenses. This led us right back to where we started, with clever CFOs being forced to mislead donors by playing games with their balance sheets and 990s.

## Spending Money to Make Money

One of the most notable takedowns of a do-gooder spending money to raise money was when Dan Pallotta's efforts to do good were thwarted.

Dan had always been involved in efforts to help others. At just 19, he became the chair of the Harvard Hunger Action Committee, raising money for Oxfam America. In the 1990s, he led a for-profit charitable company named Pallotta TeamWorks, which employed hundreds of full-time staff and raised $582 million for charities in just eight years. In 2002, with the company netting $81 million for charity after expenses (a tidy sum indeed), the company was forced to lay off its entire staff and shut its doors.

Why? Dan told the story in his now famous TED Talk which, as of this writing, has been viewed over 4 million times. Here's his explanation of what happened:

"The short story is, our sponsors split on us. They wanted to distance themselves from us because we were being crucified in the media for investing 40 percent of the gross in recruitment and customer service and the magic of the experience, and there is no accounting terminology to describe that kind of investment in growth and in the future, other than this demonic label of 'overhead.' So one day, all 350 of our great employees lost their jobs . . . because they were labeled 'overhead.' Our sponsor went and tried the events on their own. The overhead went up. Net income for breast cancer research went down by 84 percent, or 60 million dollars, in one year."

"This is what happens when we confuse morality with frugality. We've all been taught that the bake sale with five percent overhead is morally superior to the professional fundraising enterprise with 40 percent overhead, but we're missing the most important piece of information, which is: What is the actual size of these pies? Who cares if the bake sale only has five percent overhead if it's tiny? What if the bake sale only netted 71 dollars for charity because it made no investment in its scale and the professional fundraising enterprise netted 71 million dollars because it did? Now which pie would we prefer, and which pie do we think people who are hungry would prefer?"[1]

# A Broken Model

Are you getting the picture yet? At its very core, the paradigm is damaged.

Charities are saddled with extra pressure to meet formulas for how much they should spend to raise money. This policing of business practices stifles the actual mission.

Critics often preach that charities need to act more like businesses, but then they refuse to let them. In an effort to "expose fraud," critics and watchdogs impose rules regarding what amount of overhead is considered allowable. The heightened scrutiny squelches innovation in fundraising strategies, because the innovation might fail and would then be viewed as a waste of donor funds.

---

1   Dan Pallotta, "The Way We Think About Charity is Dead Wrong," TED: Ideas Worth Spreading, last modified February 2013, accessed December 2, 2017, https://www.ted.com/talks/dan_pallotta_the_way_we_think_about_charity_is_dead_wrong.

The Bridgespan Group, a global nonprofit organization that collaborates with mission-driven leaders, organizations, and philanthropists, described the situation in this graphic:

**The Bridgespan Group's depiction of the nonprofit starvation cycle.**

- **Misleading reporting:** The majority of nonprofits underreport overhead on tax forms and in fundraising materials—a result of overhead "phobia."

- **Unrealistic expectations:** Donors tend to reward organizations with the "leanest" profiles. They also skew their funding toward programmatic activities instead of overhead and innovation.

- **Pressure to conform:** Nonprofit leaders feel pressure to conform to funders' unrealistic expectations by spending as little as possible on overhead, and by reporting lower-than-actual overhead rates.

This research led me to conclude that fundraisers and donors are in a pickle. They have been unfairly subjected to a broken system for decades. It isn't their fault, but it is their problem.

I wondered . . . *Could I change the paradigm?*

# Lightning Strikes

I decided to call the diabetes charity that sent me the newsletter. After being forced to navigate a labyrinth of pages online and using their phone system, I finally reached the person responsible for using the approach. I asked her if it was working. Her answer was no.

I asked, "Do you need highly qualified leads so you can close more legacy gifts?"

She replied, "Yes."

That's when it happened. Although I'd never read a book about fundraising and was unfamiliar with its orthodoxies, I knew I could help. Thankfully, she allowed me the opportunity to do so. She gave me a shot. She let me take what I knew about marketing and human behavior to devise a campaign to garner better results.

Our first effort delivered outcomes that were simply astounding. She credited our success by writing a wonderful reference letter that said, "From virtually nonexistent leads, we have had correspondence with hundreds of individuals requesting estate planning information or stating they have left a bequest to the [organization]."

Soon after, one of the recipients of our donor-centric marketing sent it to the leadership of another diabetes charity, leading them to contact me to see if I might help them, too. Of course, I did.

I generated thousands of responses for those organizations and uncovered hundreds of bequests that were previously unknown to each of them, with a future value of almost $25 million.

I knew why my plan worked and the other one failed. It revolved around *engagement*. The confusing newsletter I originally received didn't *engage* me, for three big reasons:

1. **It was irrelevant.** I couldn't take advantage of a charitable gift annuity at the age of 37.

2. **It was impersonal.** Emotionless newsletters seemingly written by lawyers using legal jargon are uninspiring at best and off-putting at worst.

3. **It was interruptive.** Sending thousands of newsletters to donors whether they want them or not is wasteful, insensitive, and annoying to the vast majority of recipients.

I later learned that the newsletter wasn't written by anyone employed by the charity. Stressed-out fundraisers often hire outside vendors to write, design, produce, and distribute outreach communications on their nonprofit's behalf. After all, I was enlisted to generate leads for them, too.

The problem is that many of the vendors offering planned gift marketing services use cookie-cutter approaches. They simply reuse the same content for all of their clients but swap out the logos and make other customizations so their newsletters look unique.

Donors aren't fooled or inspired because most of the content is transactional in nature. These vendors tend to focus on *how* to make a legacy gift instead of engaging with each donor on a personal level about *why* they should care and how their life story entwines with the charity's mission.

The approach has been making vendors rich for decades, but it's not effective. Even so, busy fundraisers fall into the trap of doing what their predecessor did simply because that's the way it's always been done. It's an easy answer, but the presumed "experts" deliver lackluster results.

What most organizations need is major and legacy gift lead generation along with discovery of previously undisclosed legacy gifts—something very similar to what MarketSmart was already doing for private-sector businesses. Applying MarketSmart's engagement strategy brought astounding results.

So I decided to shift my business. We reengineered my marketing firm to help more charities properly engage supporters, generate highly qualified leads, cultivate those leads, and uncover hidden legacy gifts. I soon realized that we needed software to support our efforts. Since that software didn't exist, we took on the challenge and built it ourselves. Now we're helping nonprofits around the world raise more money at lower costs while providing donors with the value they deserve.

Our model is *Engagement Fundraising*—a term I developed in 2012.

# Introducing Engagement Fundraising

At its core, Engagement Fundraising is simple. It boils down to making people feel good.

It's about people, not money. It's about conversations, not transactions. It's about collaboration, not exclusion. It's about gratitude, not thanklessness. It's about fairness, not trickery.

Consider that giving has been stuck at 2 percent of Gross Domestic Product for almost half a century and the average nonprofit's first-time donor retention rate is only 32 percent (just 17 percent for new donors giving under $100).

Knowing those two statistics, one should start to wonder: If the rate of giving has stayed the same, where have the donors gone if they haven't stuck with your charity?

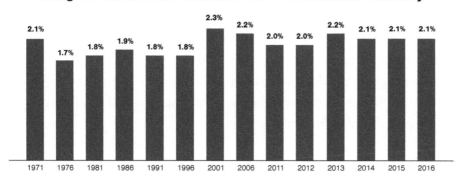

**Giving has been stuck at around 2% for almost half a century.**

Source: The Giving Institute™

I know the answer. They're hopping from one charity to another! Why? Because they want to give! They need to give! They are required to give! They love to give because it makes them feel good!

Unfortunately, donors aren't getting any love back from the nonprofit sector, and that's why they shop around, giving money to one charity this year and another the next. They're hopping and they're hoping. Hoping that they'll finally find a home with a charity that loves them back. Hoping they'll finally find a charity that thanks them with genuine sincerity. Hoping they'll finally find a charity that reports what they did with the money. Hoping they'll finally find a charity that doesn't treat them like ATM machines. Hoping they'll finally find a charity that engages with them.

Supporters want to be engaged. They want to be involved. They want to be captivated and engrossed in your mission. The best way to do all this is by harnessing smart strategy with the power of technology to provide scale and efficiency that simply weren't possible until now.

Back when I first began to study the sector, I'd ask myself, "Why are fundraisers still 'spraying and praying,' using direct mail and spam aimed at people who could care less? Why aren't they gaining permission from their audiences, allowing them to opt in and out? Why aren't they moving into the modern world and leveraging technology to target a more suitable audience, provide more relevant engagement experiences, and lower their costs?"

Engagement Fundraising addresses all of these issues and places trust at the cornerstone of its foundation. Once you gain the trust of a potential prospect, words and images have tremendous power. One of the reasons I was drawn to marketing in the first place was that I particularly liked feeling that I could influence people to do things that were good for *them*. I was starting to realize that I might influence people to do good for others, too, if I could apply these ideas in the context of fundraising.

Transparency, honesty, collaboration, and consideration: there's a reason they work in the business world, and it's the same reason they work in the charitable sector. I maintain that my early success in marketing and advertising was not because I was the best con artist. It was because I'd internalized these concepts and implemented them routinely. As you will soon see, the overarching lesson is that making people feel good generates returns.

In the 21st century, the key lies in leveraging technology to help more people feel good so they'll give money to help make the world a better place. That requires finding people who can make major gifts and then giving them a home charity that sincerely appreciates *them*, not just their donations.

Leaving a charity in one's will, or making any large gift, is a highly considered decision. It's much different from throwing change in a bucket at the grocery store—an impulse decision. With Engagement Fundraising, seeking a considered gift is all about providing valuable content and a feedback loop.

Content is an offer; it helps to engage people, entertain them, inform them, and bring out their emotions. If you create valuable content and you engage the right audience, you'll help people move themselves through the decision-making process so they'll take action. Valuable content is nonthreatening, permission oriented, considerate, and fair.

Engagement Fundraising strategically delivers valuable content to a prospective donor, they opt in, and a relationship forms with a two-way conversation thanks to a feedback loop. When a supporter accepts your valuable content, he'll often reciprocate. Sometimes he'll share information about himself. Sometimes he'll give money. Or perhaps he'll involve others. At this stage, it's best to entice him to "talk" to you through his engagement so you can grow the relationship by listening and responding to his very specific needs.

Supporters want to give! They have philanthropic ambitions, but they don't want to be treated like a money machine. Since the majority of their thinking about giving occurs without the fundraiser present, Engagement Fundraising helps the fundraiser become involved in the consideration process without being in front of them. It's about engaging, not asking. It's about leveraging technologies to open up a dialogue over a period of time. It's about providing value in line with a supporter's wants, needs, and desires. It's about allowing the supporter to move *herself* to the point of making a gift, or wanting to talk to the charity to facilitate that process. In fact, if you do your Engagement Fundraising right, you may never even have to "make the ask." Imagine that!

This is a book for fundraisers, from the perspective of a donor who discovered firsthand that fundraising is broken—me! In the following chapters, I want to show you how it can be fixed, and empower you to transform your organization. With the help of cutting-edge technology, you will be able to raise more money for your mission at lower costs, by targeting the donors most likely to deliver large, major gifts, including legacy gifts. You'll bring your organization into the 21st century, and the results will speak for themselves: happier donors, successful fundraising campaigns, and more change in the world.

## Before We Go Any Further…

Are you sure you want this? Some people don't. They're stuck. They're closed-minded. They're mired in orthodoxy, tradition, and conventions that impede progress for the human race. And, yes! I truly believe they're obstructing a revolution.

I'm a crusader and disruptor. I break things in order to rebuild them better than they once were—more efficient and more effective. I have long studied and admired other crusaders and disruptors. Their pictures adorn the walls of my firm, such as Martin Luther King, Jr., Mahatma Gandhi, Golda Meir, Nelson Mandela, and Steve Jobs. I know, however, that disruption makes people uncomfortable.

Soon after my success with the first two charities, I offered to speak at a local fundraising conference. There, I began to tell the attendees about our strategies and successes. I was excited because I felt like I'd found a cure for cancer. What happened next was entirely unexpected.

The crowd was not happy. Their arms were crossed. Their noses were turned up. The vibe was cold and uncomfortable. I was interrupted and heckled. My ideas were met with resistance and disdain.

The following week, the event coordinator called to tell me that the organizing committee had never gotten complaints about speakers before—until now. It was awful. I felt like I got punched in the face and sent to an alternate universe, one where success meant failure and results invoked contempt, derision, and scorn.

That's when I came to the conclusion that *fundraising is broken*. That's right, I said it!

I hope you're not offended by my crassness. Instead, I hope you, too, are tired of the way things are—because within these pages you'll find what my allies have already discovered: the recipe for building endowments while lowering fundraising costs so nonprofits can ensure that their missions remain funded for generations to come.

# Part One
# A New World

# Chapter 1
# The World
# Has Changed

The world of fundraising is facing a climate change. The environment is shifting and a course correction is needed. Unfortunately, fundraisers aren't keeping up.

At a fundraising conference, I once listened to a roundtable discussion that was punctuated by the "oohs" and "ahhs" of the audience. The saleswoman leading the conversation was continually highlighting the high open-rate percentage of her cookie-cutter email marketing product.

Open rates are calculated by dividing the number of email messages sent by the total number of emails opened. There are conflicting views regarding their use as a performance measure. The truth is that open rates are "vanity metrics." They don't account for the effectiveness, or ineffectiveness, of email marketing. Measuring them provides little useful information, because the number of emails viewed or opened is rarely accurate. And even if it is precise, does it matter? These days, don't we open emails repeatedly as we thumb through messages on our phones whenever we have time to spare?

Was this the next "shiny new object" that would help the fundraisers exceed their numbers? Actually no, but they thought it just might be. They wanted the product the saleswoman was describing because they were misled into thinking that open rates matter. The product was designed to appeal to busy fundraisers, but its tools and messages did just the opposite for its targets—the donors. Even worse, the saleswoman had no idea that the product she was selling didn't really work. She was pitching a *tool* for fundraisers, not something designed to help donors achieve their philanthropic dreams.

The vendor probably landed a new client or two that day because the fundraisers were blind to the fact that focusing on open rates is a waste of time. It wasn't their fault; they didn't know what they didn't know. The vendor should have known better.

The situation I witnessed around open rates is just an example of what's happening in the business of fundraising. More and more silver bullets and new whiz-bang methods of doing things keep popping up. The industry is awash in misinformation about the best marketing techniques spewed by uninformed "experts" more interested in their own gains than they are in the donors who support the charities desperately in need of their help.

I've quizzed self-proclaimed experts including thought leaders, authors, speakers, and consultants. I've discovered that too many have very little understanding of how to use marketing communications to raise major gifts (including planned gifts). I've also seen far too many nonprofit staff approve or reject marketing communications based on *their* preferences, not their donors'. Too often they're more interested in winning the internal political argument than getting results by making donors feel good. I've even witnessed the approval of communications based on what a decision maker's daughter thought as a result of her recently acquired college degree.

What you really need to know as a fundraiser is that engagement, value, and two-way conversation are the true game changers. When combined with new scientific findings, technologies, and tactics proven effective over time, results increase exponentially.

Instead of asking about open rates, you should be asking more important questions: Do donors engage? Do they click? Do they go to the web page? Do they fill out a form, donate, sign up, or involve themselves in something? Have they been enabled to effect change and find meaning in their lives? And most importantly, have they been made to feel good?

The climate change in fundraising requires not only an understanding of philosophies of engagement but also an understanding of the *appropriate* use of technology. My dad used to tell me, "Technology is just a tool, and tools can be dangerous." He'd continue, "Some people use hammers to build stuff, while others use them to break stuff." And finally he'd challenge me by asking, "What will you do with your tools?"

When used correctly, new technologies can save money, create relationships, and respect the time and interests of potential donors. However, swapping technology such as email in spray-and-pray campaigns as a replacement for direct mail can also create the same one-way, one-size-fits-all, arm's-length, donor anonymity that your supporters want you to overcome.

Historically, giving was accomplished on a one-to-one basis within the community. The fundraiser knew the donor and would personally thank them for their help. Now, a charity may have 433,612 donors. The donor may have become a segment, a target, a persona, or simply Donor I.D. A23986.

Fundraisers like you are in a difficult spot. You're constantly being asked to raise more money by your board of directors, but you don't have the staff, resources, or tools to do it the right way. You're probably overworked and underpaid. You may be patient, empathetic to your cause, and full of good intentions. You know you need to create relationships and speak to donors one-to-one, but all too often, the demands of the position force you or your marketing staff to communicate one-to-many. Generic, impersonal, one-way communications may be easier for your nonprofit to distribute and may provide short-term gains, but it doesn't pay off in the long run. It is ultimately disrespectful to donors, forcing them to hop around in search of a better experience.

# A Cautionary Tale

The story of Olive Cooke illustrates what can happen when regard for the donor is lost in a never-ending chase for the next donation. Mrs. Cooke, a 92-year-old resident of Great Britain, received an estimated 3,000 mailings from charities annually. She was featured in a newspaper article about the state of charitable fundraising six months before taking her own life. While Mrs.

Cooke's family doesn't blame the charities for her death, they are critical of the fundraising techniques they witnessed.

The Fundraising Standards Board (FRSB), an independent self-regulator for charity fundraising in the UK, stepped in to investigate after receiving hundreds of complaints related to Mrs. Cooke's story. The FSRB found that of the 99 charities possessing her information, 70 of them had acquired her personal details from someone other than Mrs. Cooke. This means that the majority of the charities marketing to Mrs. Cooke bought her contact information from other charities, and 24 continued to profit by selling it to others. Mrs. Cooke donated to 88 of the charities in her lifetime, but only 16 regularly gave her an opportunity to opt out of further communication or data sharing.

The charities cited in the report had no way of knowing the cumulative impact of their methods, but the sheer number of requests was overwhelming. The mass-marketing techniques, coupled with data sharing and the inability to opt out, led to a total disregard for Mrs. Cooke in an effort to eke out another few pounds.

The FRSB's report called for a behavioral shift within charities and a new commitment to donors based on greater respect. The report made 17 recommendations for changes to the Code of Fundraising Practice, including a requirement to include the ability to opt out of further communication, and to obtain explicit permission before sharing data.

I bet there are many Mrs. Cookes around the world today. Even with a fundraiser's good intentions, there's always a temptation to raise a few more dollars by blasting one more email. It's too easy to buy cold email lists, append your current database, and spam people you don't know.

I believe a reckoning day is coming for the rest of us, just as it did in the UK. The charitable world has changed due to technology and donor expectations. If you can embrace the change and use it to your benefit by engaging with givers in a respectful, mutually beneficial, and two-sided conversation, revolutionary results can be accomplished. If not, the storm clouds gathering on the horizon will eventually force a change, whether you're ready or not.

## The Old Models—And Why They Don't Work

Change is hard. It's even harder when you're underpaid, under-resourced, and charged with the roles most important to the mission: finding and retaining donors, raising major donations, and inspiring legacy gifts. Even so, you need to move away from traditional models to employ new ways of connecting to donors with sincerity.

Given all of the resources and time in the world, you'd probably default to the Golden Rule and have no problem treating donors as you'd like to be treated. Like dating, you would build a slow and steady relationship with a potential donor. Maybe share ideas, learn her story, understand why she cares, and gauge where she is in the consideration process before pushing her too far too fast. Instead, the time-and-money crunch forces you to fall back on old ways of doing things.

The challenge of marketing to donors is further complicated by the mindset of many fundraisers themselves that have an aversion to viewing themselves as marketers or salespeople. I even heard one Chief Development Officer take it a step further and say, "I'm not a salesperson. I'm not a marketer. I'm not even a fundraiser. I'm a dream maker!" She wanted to see herself as a do-gooder. Perhaps she felt the other descriptors were beneath her?

Here's the thing: "Sales" isn't a dirty word. It's not about being a "shark." The best salespeople are actually enormously thoughtful and kindhearted. They always aim for a win-win even though they're under pressure to generate results, too.

It seems that many fundraisers think of salespeople in the for-profit world as used car peddlers, but that simply isn't the case. The raising of money by charities is no different from sales and marketing in the private sector. A win-win is essential. When you learn to view the whole process simply, as a way to align an individual's need with what you have to offer, everyone gets the results they desire.

Sales leaders know that everything I'm describing in this book applies to them, too. The private sector is way ahead of nonprofits in this regard, which makes sense. Their profit model financially motivates them—their CEOs, managers, and salespeople—to crack the code on what truly works and what doesn't. If they don't, their investors seek change. In the 21st century, your investors (your donors) will, too.

# The Pyramid

Still reading? Terrific. But get ready for some turbulence. I'm about to shatter some traditions, orthodoxies, and conventions that many fundraisers hold on to for dear life. Let's begin.

When we talk about old models, one of the most timeworn fundraising concepts is the donor pyramid model, perhaps because it offers an alternative to the traditional sales and marketing funnel method of moving leads to qualified prospects and then to customers. I can only assume that the pyramid model was first developed because, in the past, fundraisers generally didn't want to be thought of as marketers or salespeople. But, as I've previously mentioned—they are. Almost every exchange of money for value involves marketing and selling. Fundraising is simply a subset of that archetype, not a separate category.

When organizations embrace the traditional fundraising pyramid, they try to acquire donors at the bottom of the pyramid, usually aiming to gain donations from low-level, first-time donors. Any donation is enough in this model, because it enables entry into the process. Fundraisers then try to move donors up the pyramid, perhaps first pursuing monthly, repeat donations.

Then they'll try to inspire larger and larger gifts until the donor reaches the midlevel category. Usually, the midlevel is where things get messy. The supporter who gave 25 bucks a month is now giving $500 here and there. They've moved themselves from "coach" to "business class," but they usually don't get treated any better. In fact, many midlevel donors end up not getting any communication at all.

Since midlevel-category donors usually aren't worthy of costly face-to-face relationships with Major Gift Officers and no longer fit in the lower level, they often get ignored and then stop giving altogether. Then they hop away looking for a charity that will love them back.

If the donor somehow makes it through this maze, however, they might eventually find themselves approached by a Major Gift Officer. The Gift Officer will seek to build a relationship that might lead to greater giving in the "first class" zone.

Finally, the charity will hope for the ultimate gift: a legacy gift. Charities fail to realize that most people change their minds, removing charities from their estate plans or shifting their distribution percentages within the tempestuous last days of their lives.

Additionally, many wealthy people would rather pass their money on to their heirs, and they often say they have left a gift in their will when they haven't.

The fact is, the traditional pyramid is wrong. Legacy gifts can come from anyone, not just those moved up by the charity. The average person reserves their single most meaningful donation, their major gift, until *after* their lifetime. It might even be their first donation that the charity receives.

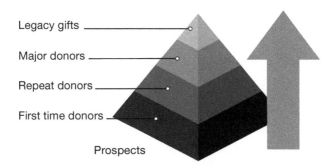

Legacy gifts
Major donors
Repeat donors
First time donors
Prospects

**Traditional fundraising pyramid.**

For decades, fundraisers have referred to these heaven-sent donations as "coming over the transom." (A transom is a window found in some old-fashioned offices that sits just above a doorway and can be opened so people can toss mail over the crossbar.) These gifts often come from donors, but they also come from advocates, members, staff, volunteers, and even people who have been following your charity's efforts on social media.

For example, there may be a donor with fond memories of her college who leaves a large gift in her will, or a donor who gives to the music society in honor of an aunt who always took her to the opera. Where do they fall on the pyramid? They don't.

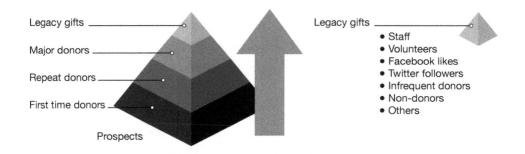

**New model recognizing that legacy gifts can come
from anyone and can be a supporter's first donation.**

Another fallacy that forms the foundation of the pyramid model is that low-dollar first-time givers will continue to give. However, data from the Fundraising Effectiveness Project shows that higher-dollar first-time givers retain at a higher rate and also repeat with larger donations.

The pyramid model defies logic once you examine the data. On average, only 17 percent of new donors giving $100 or less give again. Of that 17 percent, only 47 percent give a third time. Compare that to new donors whose first gift is between $1,000 and $5,000. Fifty-seven percent of them give again, and then give a third time at a rate of 87 percent. In other words, the first-time donors who give between $1,000 and $5,000 are more than three times more likely to give again compared with low-dollar donors and are almost twice as likely to give a third time compared to the same group.

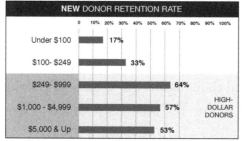
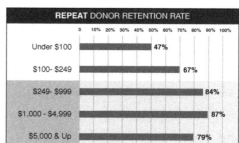

Source: Fundraising Effectiveness Project
Examination of anonymous data from 3,590 organizations thanks to their partnerships with many of the best-known software (CRM) providers. These charts represent the loyalty of donors among the top 20% fastest growing organizations in this group in 2013.

Formula: Total dollars raised in 2013 minus total dollars raised in 2010 as a percentage of total dollars raised in 2010. The AFP sponsored FEP statistics are the best available statistics for the sector. www.afpfep.org

Although it may only work for a small segment of your audience, doesn't it make sense to loosen your allegiance to the pyramid concept and target the supporters more likely to give larger amounts in the first place?

The pyramid approach is relied on as a tried-and-true method of acquiring and retaining donors. It has been the cornerstone of the old paradigm in fundraising. It may have worked when direct mail, telemarketing, and face-to-face meetings were the only channels available. Research proves that the theory doesn't live up to the hype, but the approach also doesn't reflect a spirit of partnership between the organization and the donor. Instead, the donor is treated as someone who needs to be "moved" up the pyramid.

*We can do better.* "Moving donors" sounds like it involves trickery and manipulation. It isn't the answer. The secret lies in treating a donor well and giving them what they need. When fundraising is donor-centered, donors move *themselves* up the pyramid. It's your job to help them, not "move" them.

# A Better Model

The pyramid model is outdated. It's not the way big dollars are generated in the private sector, and it doesn't work in the fundraising sector. The better approach is the traditional sales/marketing four-step funnel. Believe it or not, this funnel more accurately reflects the reality of the fundraising world. It's based on the donor as the customer and their consideration process. The pyramid cares little about the donor's timeline and thought process; it cares only about what the organization wants the donor to do. The funnel is donor-centric— and that's what this book is all about.

The marketing process, regardless of the sector, always needs to align with the buyer's or donor's consideration process. Once you understand the donor's journey, you can align your engagement messages and offers to meet the donor's needs at every stage of the consideration process.

I've seen colleges and universities target their new graduates who are faced with slim job prospects and just beginning to struggle to pay off their student loans. Those people may be happy to make a small, affordable gift, but most aren't. Then when the school continues to hound and harass them without providing value in exchange for the gifts, they get ticked off. Can you blame them?

**Traditional sales and marketing funnel.**

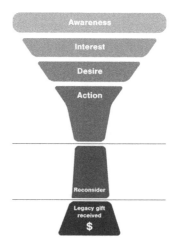

**Major and planned gift fundraising funnel.**

Instead of hounding new graduates for money, engage them. Start by providing them with offers that help them, not the school. Provide them with opportunities to find a mentor among past graduates who has already found success in their careers. Help them find and befriend other graduates in their local community with similar interests. Help them get a job. Through it all, provide them with an opportunity to benefit from something valuable you helped provide.

Don't make giving the focus of the relationship. You haven't earned their support yet. They've just spent a fortune on their education. Asking for donations or "moving them" too fast will offend them in a way they might never forgive.

## The Populist Concept

The pyramid model is heavily intertwined with the populist approach, which is based on the idea of getting as many people as possible to give—at least a little. The populist concept is widespread, and it maintains that all donors deserve the same treatment.

The populist idea has been around a long time. After all, what could possibly be wrong with a philosophy that might have started with one of the most prolific fundraisers in America, Ben Franklin? Franklin's method equates to relentless networking, and leaves no one out. He described it this way:

> In the first place, I advise you to apply to all those whom you know will give something; next to those whom you are uncertain whether they will give anything or not; and show them the list of those who have given; and, lastly, do not neglect those who you are sure will give nothing; for in some of them you may be mistaken.[2]

In Ben's day, the populist approach made sense, because there were less people to solicit and it moved charitable fundraising into the realm of societal obliga-

2 Benjamin Franklin, *The Autobiography of Benjamin Franklin: 1706-1757* (Carlisle, MA: Applewood Books, 2008), page 137.

tion and away from its reliance on the church. Even now, the intentions of the populist approach aren't bad. It's hard to argue with the attitude of inclusion and cooperation. But the inefficiency becomes obvious when you examine the practice more closely.

Fundraisers who believe in the populist approach might seek to meet a $50,000 goal by asking for and getting $50 from one thousand people, instead of $40,000 from one person, $1,000 from five people, $100 from 40 people, and the rest from twenty $50 hits. When organization leaders and their boards ask for more donors, good-hearted fundraisers flock to the populist method, thinking that if they can just double the number of givers, they will double their revenue. The appeal is even greater if those fundraisers are shying away from meeting face-to-face with individual donors. Often that drives them toward the ease of signing a purchase order to send more spam or junk mail to more people.

Populist fundraisers argue that fundraising is evolving from big donors to big networks, and they believe that marketing to the top of the pyramid hurts their nonprofit's future. They want to deliver the same communications to everyone, because they believe the small piece of their donor base that's made up of older, richer supporters is a high-risk and high-reward constituency. This notion sounds good in theory, but it just isn't true.

I'll admit that populist fundraising can be effective sometimes. For politicians, donations might equal votes, so it makes sense for them to reach out to all types of supporters to request donations. In politics, populist fundraising works and makes sense.

But fundraising for nonprofits is a business, and the most effective techniques have to be used to achieve the charity's mission at the lowest cost. Other than the example of using a populist approach in politics, treating all donors the same across the board is not the way to go. It's expensive and very hard to do in a highly personalized, engagement-oriented way.

# The Pareto Principle

It goes without saying that charities need to use smart business strategies to meet their goals. Pyramid and populist fundraising don't fit the bill because they assume all donors are created equal, and we know they aren't. Instead, you should give priority treatment to the best donors and prospects. Doesn't it make sense to use your precious time and valuable resources on finding and retaining more people who are not only passionate about your cause, but also have the capacity to make serious impact, instead of spending tons of money on low-dollar, low-capacity donors and then trying to move them up the pyramid?

The reason it makes sense to focus on the small percentage of high-value donors can be traced to an Italian economist, Vilfredo Pareto. In 1906, Pareto discovered that 80 percent of the land in Italy was owned by 20 percent of the people. He further expanded the concept by observing that 20 percent of the pea pods in his garden contained 80 percent of the peas.

The concept quickly caught on and businesses everywhere soon came to realize that 80 percent of their sales came from 20 percent of their clients. This later came to be known as the 80/20 rule.

It works for nonprofits, too. Twenty percent of your donors generally will account for 80 percent of your revenue. Quite frequently these days, closer to 10 percent account for 90 percent of your revenue.

According to the Giving USA Foundation Annual Report on Philanthropy for the Year 2016, total giving in the United States in 2016 was $390.05 billion. Of that sum, individual giving (including bequests) accounted for $312.22 billion or precisely 80.046 percent of all giving, with corporations accounting for about 5 percent ($18.55 billion) and foundations adding about 15 percent ($59.28 billion). It's funny how the Pareto principle works, isn't it?

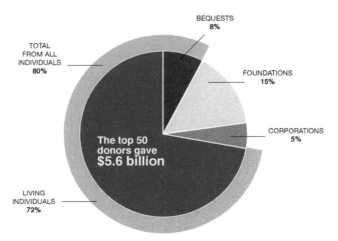

TOTAL FROM ALL INDIVIDUALS 80%

BEQUESTS 8%

FOUNDATIONS 15%

CORPORATIONS 5%

The top 50 donors gave $5.6 billion

LIVING INDIVIDUALS 72%

**Source:** Giving USA and the Chronicle of Philanthropy in 2016, the top 50 most charitable U.S. citizens gave $5.6 billion and total giving in the U.S. was $390.05 billion.

Here are some other figures to consider. Although they don't precisely match up with the 80/20 rule, they complement the point. According to the IRS reportage of form 8283 (noncash individual contribution) filings in 2010:

- .1 percent of taxpayers (3,898 reporting earnings of $10 million per year or more) accounted for 28.8 percent of the entire country's non-cash charitable donations.

- 2.9 percent of taxpayers (206,972 reporting earnings of $500,000 or more) accounted for 53.6 percent of the entire country's charitable donations.

- 14.8 percent of taxpayers (1,077,179 reporting earnings of $200,000 or more) accounted for 63.1 percent of the entire country's charitable donations.

More can be found in the 2012 Bank of America Study of High Net Worth Philanthropy, a study based on data gathered from a comprehensive survey of 20,000 high-net-worth donors in America's wealthiest neighborhoods. The study found that 3 percent of U.S. households are responsible for two-thirds of all household charity. That's pretty darn close to the 2.9 percent/53.6 percent figures reported by the IRS in 2010.

Most organizations spend their marketing dollars in direct opposition to the Pareto principle. Too often more than 80 percent of the marketing dollars get spent on acquisition fundraising aimed at gaining new low-level, low-capacity donors.

Interestingly, for-profit businesses know that the Pareto principle is essential to their success. However, as soon as their leaders get the opportunity to help their favorite charities as board members, I've heard them say things like, "We just need more new donors," or "If we could just get 5,000 new people to give $100!" It's astounding, but for some strange reason, perfectly smart business leaders lose their marbles when they enter the nonprofit universe.

Zeroing in on high-capacity (wealthy), passionate, engaged supporters to generate major gifts, including legacy gifts, is essential. One of the most fundamental strategic concepts is focusing marketing efforts and resources on the 20 percent of your donors who have the capacity and ability to make large or legacy gifts. Master this, and you will endow your nonprofit's mission with the greatest degree of efficiency at the lowest cost—period.

Here's a quick and easy way to determine if your budget is appropriated properly with the Pareto principle. Just fill in the percentages that reflect your organization's revenue sources and fundraising spending (budget).

|  | % of your fundraising REVENUE | % of your fundraising BUDGET |
|---|---|---|
| **Top of the pyramid (top 20%)** |  |  |
| **Middle of the pyramid (middle 60%)** |  |  |
| **Bottom of the pyramid (bottom 20%)** |  |  |

So, what did you determine?

Is your organization focused on the 20 percent that delivers 80 percent of your revenue? Is your budget spent on providing tremendous value to those individuals who can deliver large donations and bequests? Is it spent on helping your loyal, high-capacity donors encourage their friends to join them in supporting your mission? Is your budget focused on delivering great service to your high-value donors? Is it focused on finding more donors that model your major donors and legacy society members?

Or are you spending most of your budget on acquiring new, low-level donors who don't have enough interest, are disengaged, and lack the capacity to make impactful donations?

I'm not saying you should stop acquiring lower-level supporters. I'm not saying you should stop building awareness for your cause. I am saying you should take care of your core supporters who have the capacity to make a serious positive impact on your mission first. You should give them an unbelievable engagement experience every time they reach out to you or raise their hands showing interest. Roll out the red carpet for them and help them invite their friends to join in.

Focus your efforts by recognizing the power of the Pareto principle first. Then you'll have tons of cash to do whatever else you want to do. Spend more of your budget on less people. Deliver much more value to them and you will achieve more in less time while raising more funds at lower cost.

## Breaking the Cycle with Technology

Without innovation, nobody wins; donors, fundraisers, and beneficiaries are trapped in a cycle destined to repeat itself. Here's what it looks like: After a year or so in a position with a charity, a fundraiser moves on. Perhaps the board changes. New parties may move into the positions, but all of the players are still underpaid, and they're still under the same pressures.

Money has to be raised, and donors must be found. What's a new hire supposed to do? You'll probably feel a lot of pressure to do what's always been done because you're short on time and resources. You may be scared to try anything new in case it doesn't work and might be considered a waste of donor money. So you'll probably rely on the vendors servicing your account, just as your predecessor did. It's the path of least resistance because the only party that hasn't been involved in the revolving door of the nonprofit is the direct mail/digital vendor that offers populist fundraising or spray-and-pray services.

The losers in this self-perpetuating game are the donors, the beneficiaries, and eventually the charity. High-capacity donors want to give; it's part of their humanity. But they aren't stupid, and if they aren't getting the value they deserve, they'll eventually go looking for another charity that treats them better.

Think about it this way. We've already covered the fact that giving is stuck at 2 percent of GDP, and most organizations have a low rate of retention. We've figured out that donors are hopping around, hoping to find a charity that makes them feel appreciated, valued, and involved—a place that takes them out of the endless cycle of pitches for more donations and makes them feel *good!*

Isn't it time you utilized technology to help you break the cycle? Technology has been the key for innovation in the private sector, and technology can provide the keys to finding and retaining your "Pareto" top 20 percent. The systemic problems prevalent in the nonprofit sector can be overcome, and the good news is that it won't require adding more staff or paying them more money so they stick around longer (although that's not a bad thing).

Leveraging technology will help you save time and money as it enables you to focus on the top-level givers for your organization. For example, relevant online communities and big data are a source of finding donors, and technology offers opportunities for easier tracking that weren't possible before. Add some artificial intelligence and machine learning and you'll be gaining ground on how for-profit businesses leverage technology to garner greater results. But I'm getting ahead of myself here. More on all that later.

The real benefit of technology, however, is that it enables you to deliver amazing, personalized experiences to supporters and relate with them in more meaningful ways individually. Using technology to engage prospects allows you to learn what they want and need, and to monitor their involvement to determine where they are in the gift consideration process. Ultimately, technology can put you in the right place at the right time—precisely when the donor wants you there to facilitate their giving and make them feel good.

Technology provides convenience. After all, that's the number-one reason why people use Amazon to buy their stuff. Uber, Tesla, Apple, and others have shown the rest of us the way. It's time for the nonprofit sector to follow their path by using technology to determine with whom to engage, when to engage, what to say in your communications, and why your prospects even care about giving. Best of all, you can use technology to capture and provide all of this information, with the added benefit of building trust.

Fundraising is like a big game of musical chairs. Donors are going to sit with the charity that engages them properly and makes them feel good. People with capacity crave engagement. Their desire for your outreach is pent up. It's as simple as asking them how they feel, why they donated, and how they want to be involved with your mission. Once you know the answers, it's about showing them that you listened by providing them with opportunities for engagement that suits their needs. Doing it this way will ingratiate you to them. They'll be more likely to meet you. They'll be more likely to be open with you. They'll be more likely to work with you to realize their philanthropic aspirations.

Gone are the days of donors making a gift and trusting the process. Donor expectations have changed, because donors can self-inform, self-qualify, self-involve, and even self-solicit. A smart fundraiser will realize this and use technology to make valuable offers, involve prospects on their own terms, and create personal relationships. Donors will get the experience they deserve, and charities will raise more money that can be used for good.

# Chapter 2
# Donor Expectations Have Changed

When I first got into professional sales at the age of 14, I was taught that the only way to sell anything was to get face-to-face with a prospect. I walked up and down the streets of my neighborhood knocking on doors and ringing bells asking anyone who opened their door if they wanted their car washed and waxed. That was my first business! By getting face-to-face, my batting average was pretty good.

I later sold advertising space for a newspaper by walking into retail stores at strip malls and asking for the owner or manager. My next gig was at an ad agency that focused on direct mail marketing for nonprofits in the D.C. region. We had one computer in the office that everyone shared to type and print out personal letters. My job was to generate new business. In order to get face-to-face with prospects downtown, I made cold calls to set appointments for meetings using the telephone. I figure I made about 30,000 cold calls in those days and I kept track of my "moves" with four-by-six-inch index cards and a pen. There was no internet and no email. This was in 1994.

Guess what? It isn't 1994 anymore. Technologies have changed and so have buyer and donor expectations. People no longer want to engage with brands, companies, salespeople, nonprofits, and fundraisers in the same way they used to. Now people want to (and can) have control by going online before doing anything else.

Believe it or not, closing a major or legacy gift is a lot like selling a car these days. The average price of a new car in the U.S. right now is equal to a decent-sized major gift or bequest—just below $35,000.

In the past, the only way you could buy a car was to visit a dealer and talk to a salesperson. Once there, you could gather information. Although buying a car was something you did every few years or so, the salesperson sold cars every day. He became very skilled after meeting with hundreds of people over time and learning all the ways to command the situation. It was a terrible, anxiety-inducing experience for the buyer because sorely needed information and experience were in the hands of the seller.

Automobile dealers no longer hold the cards in this way. They don't expect buyers to walk in to gather the information they need from a face-to-face chat with a salesperson. Instead, they recognize that 99 percent of all buyers go online first before making their way in for a visit. At times that are convenient for them, they'll search for information to support their decision to move themselves to the next step of the consideration process or take action.

There's still lots of brand advertising on TV, but the real action happens online. They'll explore sites that help them compare the options. They'll play with apps and widgets that help them design a car that matches their tastes and needs. Then, once the dealer has their contact information, a free gift card might be offered to entice them to visit and take a test drive. When the buyer is ready, they'll finally visit the dealer to facilitate their transaction. Today, the best facilitators win.

It isn't much different for fundraisers. The ways you and your nonprofit once connected with donors have evolved, and so have donors' expectations. What used to work—signing purchase orders—may be the easiest course of action for busy fundraisers these days, but it simply won't help you build scale for massive revenue in a cost-efficient manner.

Remember when wealthy donors had to meet with a Gift Officer in person in order to find out what was going on at the charity or make a gift? Today, it may not only be unnecessary, but also unwanted. Here are a few reasons why:

- Donors are busy and time is their most valuable asset.

- They have tools to help them educate themselves using smartphones, tablets, and computers at a time of their choosing.

- They don't want to be pressured, shamed, or made to feel uncomfortable in any way.

- They might not like the fundraiser and prefer to build a relationship with the mission and their impact, not the representative for whom they have an aversion.

- They have had a new Gift Officer reach out to them every 18 months or so as a result of high turnover at the nonprofit.

- They can give using their donor-advised fund (sometimes anonymously) or a trust.

- They can give conveniently online; $10,000 or $25,000 gifts are being made via credit card at a growing rate.

These changes put fundraisers in a tough spot. Under intense pressure to raise more and more money in less time, it's hard to be strategic and imaginative. Prospects don't accept their calls or won't take meetings.

If the big donations you need require time and relationship building, and donors don't want to meet face-to-face as much as they used to, what are you supposed to do?

Understanding what donors want and expect these days is the first step. Next, you need to build trust by providing a tremendous amount of value to the donor before you can ask for a face-to-face meeting. Value can come in many forms and is in the eye of the beholder. You need to understand what your donors want so you can give it to them.

The best way to reinforce your efforts to build trust is to adopt an attitude of *giving* to the donor with no expectation of getting anything in return. It boggles my mind when I hear fundraisers say, "Always ask for the gift!" with no thought about whether or not they've given any value to the donor first and often. Fundraisers need to be fair, respectful, and kind. They need to give before they can receive.

## LEARN > GIVE > ASK

First, take the time to learn why people care. Once you understand why they want to give, adopt a giving mindset. It's only after you give things of value to a donor that you may be in the position to ask for money.

Finally, fundraisers must use new technologies to build that trust and open up the channels of communication cost-efficiently while making engagement nonthreatening, easy, and convenient for the donor. As trust grows and your donors involve themselves more with your mission and your gifts, you'll need to track them to prioritize who is ready for outreach. This will allow you to determine who actually wants a deeper, more personal relationship with you and your organization. I expand on this later in the book.

# You Have Competition

Donors are customers. It will serve you well if you treat them as such for three big reasons. First, charities have tremendous competition from other charities. According to the National Philanthropic Trust, the number of public charities (501(c)(3)) in the U.S. has grown from 721,456 in 2001 to 1,521,052 in 2015. That's nothing short of explosive thanks to passionate individuals and families trying to save the world—usually from headquarters at their own kitchen tables. It's never been easier to start a new charity and begin asking for donations from one's friends and community.

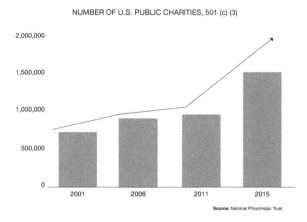

NUMBER OF U.S. PUBLIC CHARITIES, 501 (c) (3)

Source: National Philantropic Trust

**Since 2001 the U.S. has experienced explosive growth
in the number of U.S. public charities.**

Second is the growth of donor-advised funds (DAF) that are used mostly by wealthier charitable people to fund their philanthropic interests. A DAF is a way for high-capacity donors to make an irrevocable gift, take the immediate tax benefit, and then transfer the fund's dollars to any qualified charity at later dates.

Donor-advised funds are popular because they are easier to create and manage than a foundation. Big financial firms such as Fidelity or Schwab, and small ones such as your local community foundation, can become a sponsor to help create a donor-advised fund for anyone who has money and an interest in giving to charity.

From 2010 to 2016, the number of donor-advised fund accounts grew from 184,364 to 284,965, and the value of the assets in those funds grew from $33.60 billion to $$85.15 billion. The average account size has been hovering around $300,000. That means more and more wealthy people are choosing to move their dollars into donor-advised funds. They're electing to make grants to charities remotely and often anonymously, which makes it harder for fundraisers to engage with them or even know who they are.

| Number of fund accounts | 184,364 | 284,965 |
|---|---|---|
| Average account size | $169,636 | $298,809 |
| Total value of contributions | $9.35 billion | $23.27 billion |
| Total value of assets | $33.60 billion | $85.15 billion |
| Total granted to charities | $7.24 billion | $15.75 billion |
| | **2010** | **2016** |

Source: National Philanthropic Trust

**From 2010 to 2016 the number of donor-advised fund accounts grew by almost 55%.**

The third reason is obvious but often forgotten. The private sector is always competing with your nonprofit for a "share of wallet," and they're investing heavily in providing customer-service experiences to drive satisfaction. The private sector recognizes that their customers (your donors) respond to and deserve the "Disney experience." They show their approval for the private sector's investments in delivering value with their wallets and prove their displeasure with their feet.

The Disney experience translates into exceptional service that builds loyalty, retention, and profits. Disney is great at connecting with its customers. Disney does whatever it can to learn if you have boys, or girls, or both. It engages with prospective customers to learn their names and ages. It knows when it's more appropriate to send you an offer to consider a Disney Cruise, as compared with an offer for Disney World. It sends marketing aimed at your children and you, often using your names directly on their communications. It learns whether some customers want to stay on the property, and it learns which people should be engaged with less expensive offers. It learns which characters will resonate with which kids and tailors its mailings appropriately.

More importantly, all of the Disney experience is a result of powerful two-way conversations. Disney asks in ways that invite high response rates, it listens, and then it engages in highly relevant, highly contextual, highly personalized ways that meet needs and delights customers.

You may have noticed that Disney has trained its staff to listen carefully for customer needs. I'll never forget when I spent a fortune to take my family to Disney World in Florida one summer. It was hot and humid. The lines were terribly long and my wife and young kids were uncomfortable and unhappy.

The day was passing us by and we were finally getting on a ride after waiting over an hour. My son was sweating bullets. With tears in his eyes, he turned to me and said, "Dad, it's almost three o'clock and this is only our third ride."

Seconds later, a "cast member" tugged on my shirt just as we were about to take our seats. Her eyes were filled with compassion and she said, "Sir, I am so sorry. Can I speak with you for a very brief moment? I'd really like to give you and your family a very special present."

How could I resist? We stepped out of line and she apologized again by first saying she was sorry for listening in to our conversation but it's important to her and everyone working there that we have an amazing experience, and it sounded like that wasn't happening. Then she handed us special V.I.P. passes that allowed us to go to the front of the line for every ride for the remainder of the day.

I was so happy I almost cried. We jumped on that ride and tore through several others before leaving the park absolutely ecstatic about the experience. Disney listened. They provided value that met our needs. They earned our trust and our dollars.

Are you providing that level of service to your supporters? If not, the competition might eat you alive.

## Give Them a Feedback Loop

Disney also places staff near the exits of their parks to ask for feedback. If you agree to provide it, they'll usher you into a special room to take a survey.

When you're in the beginning stages of planning a trip, they also collect information from you. They wisely provide value in order to gain your trust and entice you to give them the information they need to satisfy your needs. For instance, they offer helpful planning tools in order to gain information about you, your family, your desires, and your needs. Once they have that information, they "speak" to you in a highly relevant manner using email, regular mail, or other channels you've approved for their outreach. Usually their communications include your names and reflect what you told them.

Once you've planned your trip (and forked over your money) prior to a visit, Disney uses the information they collected to provide you with more outstanding service such as tips to avoid long lines or gain memorable experiences with your favorite characters. In fundraising, we call that stewardship. It's not rocket science. But it does require smart thinking, intuitive planning, and tremendous diligence.

Are you providing your prospects and supporters with a Disney experience? What do you really know about them? Are you listening to them? Have you opened up channels of communication for dialogue? Are you making it easy for them to engage with you?

Listening and responding appropriately is the foundation of two-way conversation. Dialogue helps build trust and deliver value. Focusing only on asking donors to give without providing exceptional value doesn't work and depletes trust. You can combat this growing mistrust, however, by showing each donor that you are sincerely interested in what they need and think.

Creating a dialogue—a feedback loop—requires donor participation and involvement, as well as your ability to use the information you collect to further build the relationship. You have to truly want to learn about a donor's interests, needs, hopes, and desires. You have to listen and engage. You have to be real and sincere.

# Surveys

Surveys are one of the best ways to start to understand your prospect and facilitate an authentic connection. At MarketSmart, we felt so strongly that surveys were necessary that we created the ultimate donor survey platform in order to help fundraisers collect information from supporters.

Surveys are powerful because most supporters are starving for an opportunity to engage more deeply by providing feedback to their favorite causes. An experienced fundraising consultant once told me, "If you want advice, ask for money; but if you want money, ask for advice."

At MarketSmart, we use the survey to collect two valuable pieces of information: *verbatims* and *digital body language*. *Verbatims* are the exact words your prospects and supporters use to tell you why they care and who they want to honor or commemorate, as well as their interests, needs, hopes, and desires. *Digital body language* consists of online engagement behavior such as email clicks, page views, time-on-site, frequency of visits, etc.

Verbatims are what your donors tell you. Digital body language is the truth serum, since people don't always say what they mean. For instance, most donors will say that tax breaks for giving do not inspire them to give. Their online activity, however, sometimes tells a different story. By tying a donor's online engagements to their donor ID, we might see the same donor click on information about tax deductions online.

Although nonprofits can cobble together many technologies today to capture verbatims and digital body language and tie the information to individual donor records (by name), I'm proud to say that MarketSmart is the only provider of a platform that captures this treasure trove of information. Gathering this kind of 360-degree understanding of your supporters is key to raising more money faster.

Remember, the point of getting the information "straight from the horse's mouth" is to understand their life story and why they care, how they want to be asked or not asked, how they want to give, etc. This feedback can be used for prioritizing and/or targeting your marketing efforts so you can be more efficient and more effective. Surveys work because they make donors feel good and involved. But they work better when you use the information to engage further in an authentic, highly personalized, highly relevant, highly contextual manner that shows your supporters that you listened and you care about them as much as they care about your mission.

Being "real," being transparent, and being open and honest about your organization's efforts (both the successes and the failures) will help you build trust. Trust leads to commitment. Then it leads to retention, loyalty, major gifts, and planned gifts. True transparency in Engagement Fundraising includes such things as regular updates that provide value to donors by involving them with impact results and sharing stories from the field.

By continuously asking for their feedback and delivering value based on what they say, donors will feel like real insiders. For example, if a donor invests in (or is interested in investing in) a new hospital wing, let them see the architectural plans or a video about the building and let them tell their story to you about why they might invest. Give them a chance to select rooms they'd like to name in honor of loved ones. Most of all, make it easy and convenient for them to "talk" to you whether it's by telephone, email, or online using social media or surveys.

# Tips for Creating Surveys

Surveys work. They've worked since 800 A.D. when many believe Charles the Great conducted the first survey to understand crucial issues in his kingdom, and they work now.

The reason surveys are so beneficial is that they provide feedback to help you adjust and course-correct. With the appropriate feedback, you can prioritize and craft your marketing efforts so you can be more donor-centric.

Supporters like surveys. They want to be engaged, involved, and feel like their input counts. If done correctly, a survey will make your donors feel valued and give your nonprofit numerous benefits, such as: raising more money, identifying your 80/20, finding volunteers or new major donors, recruiting board members, monitoring trends, and uncovering previously hidden planned gifts, among others.

If surveys are good for your charity and good for your donors, what's stopping you? Don't know what questions to ask or what words work best? Don't know how to design a survey? Don't have the technological capability? Don't worry! If you want to get the most out of your survey efforts, follow these tips:

1. **Be strategic. Set clear goals for your survey by considering:**

   a. Why are you doing it?

   b. What do you aim to accomplish?

   c. Who are the stakeholders?

   d. What will you do with the information?

2. **Be donor-centric.**

   a. Limit the number of questions (10 or less).

   e. Only ask questions that are absolutely necessary to attain the objective.

   c. Be honest and up front.

d. Use simple words and short sentences (avoid jargon and long paragraphs no matter how highly educated you think your audience is).

e. Design it so it's easy to complete on desktop, mobile, or tablet devices and in print.

f. Always use big fonts in dark colors on light backgrounds with easy-to-click buttons.

g. Make sure the flow seems logical.

h. Allow supporters the opportunity to come back to an incomplete survey using cookie-based tracking technologies.

i. Put related questions in groups and describe what those groups are.

j. Employ a progress bar so people know how many questions they have answered and how many remain.

k. Avoid "requiring" questions to be answered before continuing unless absolutely necessary.

l. Use mostly closed-ended questions so your donors don't have to think too much. For example, in the case of a hair salon:

GOOD: Which of our services do you use? Massage | Hair | Stylist | Nails

BAD: What do you like about our salon?

NOTE: You may use open text boxes for elaboration, but do so sparingly. Long-form answers require more thought, energy, and time.

3. **Ways to increase your completion rates.**

   a. Tell them why you need their input and explain how your organization will benefit in a way that also benefits the respondent.

   b. Explain why you selected the respondent to answer the survey.

   c. Tell them that their opinion matters and could make a difference.

   d. Start with easy and interesting questions to get them in the groove, and then progress to greater complexity (but never too challenging!).

   e. Use the word "you" to emphasize that you're focused on them.

   f. Create a sense of urgency by mentioning that you need their response by a specific date.

   g. For sensitive questions, be sure to explain why you're asking the question and provide options so your supporters don't feel boxed in. For example: Not applicable, Prefer not to answer, Comments.

   h. Make sure your survey is branded so your supporters feel it's trustworthy and credible. NOTE: Services such as Survey Monkey can't do this, and using low-end services will result in drastically reduced completion rates.

   i. Include your contact information so they can reach out to you directly (phone and email of a real person along with a link to your website).

   f. Include your privacy policy (especially as it relates to the information you're collecting).

   g. Wait to put any demographic check boxes near the end.

h. Employ back-end form filling to get them to hit Submit. In other words, fill the last page with information you already know about them such as name, address, phone number, email address, etc. This way they don't have to spend time typing in all of the information you already have/should already know. NOTE: MarketSmart employs this technology for clients.

i. Allow them to update their contact information so your follow-up outreach is successful.

## 4. Before the survey.

Prepare for the responses by training staff (create cheat sheets for what to say to whom based on the response you might anticipate receiving), and involving departments (let everyone know what's happening so they aren't surprised by calls or emails).

## 5. After the survey.

a. Provide valuable offers to the respondents. Make sure they're relevant and personalized based on their needs and desires described in their responses (this is done most easily online). For example, provide opportunities for respondents to sign up for newsletters and/or alerts, help them send a letter to their member of Congress, allow them a chance to donate immediately or through their donor-advised funds, and offer information (ebooks or downloads) that align with their self-described desires.

b. Give them a chance to share their story with you, or spread information about your mission.

c. Respond to everyone but prioritize them by first reaching out to the people who seem to have issues or problems that need to be resolved right away.

d. Analyze the data to determine whether your survey helped you achieve your strategic objectives.

e.  Determine the next steps!

f.  Set meetings with passionate, high-capacity prospects and planned-giving leads. Steward new legacy society members.

g.  Reach out to referrals.

h.  ENGAGE!

# What Donors Want

So, what exactly do donors really want?

## The Ability to Grant Permission

There's a funny thing about vampires. They must be invited into a home or they simply can't go in. Strange, right? Interestingly, before a victim might potentially succumb to the vampire's mystical powers, they need to offer an invitation.

I'm not saying that fundraisers are vampires aiming to harm donors. We all know fundraisers just want to help donors realize their philanthropic interests. But there's something to be learned from the analogy.

Donors will be exponentially more likely to grant you power if you ask their permission to engage. They expect to have the power to reject you first. They want the opportunity to opt in or opt out of the conversation. Why not give it to them?

By opting in, the donor grants you mystical powers. Then it's up to you to further build their trust after you clear that first hurdle. Donor surveys, and other opportunities for donors to provide feedback or involve themselves, only work well if donors have the ability to grant you permission to continue the dialogue after they've leaned in.

Remember, supporters engage, volunteer, advocate, join, and give to satisfy *their* needs, not yours. But you might say, "We don't want to give them the opportunity to opt out. We'll lose people from our list." My answer is always that if they don't want to be on your list, let them go! Otherwise, you'll make them mad. Imprisoning them never works. Tightening your grip with interruptions and harassment won't inspire more donations. Instead, it will ensure defections.

If they want to go, let them move on while you do the same. It's not about having a big list; it's about having a list that's highly qualified. Less is more. Quality over quantity.

If your board is concerned that your list is shrinking, perhaps the board needs to be educated that they're focusing on the wrong numbers. Share with them the level of participation among those who fit the 80/20 rule and opted in along with how highly engaged they are. Share the growth in time they've spent on your site. Share the number of highly qualified leads you've acquired, the amounts of donations attained, and the levels of retention you've gained. Always focus on engagement and revenue metrics, not vanity metrics such as list size.

Use the Pareto principle. Seek to grow your list with people who want to be on it, who are highly engaged, and who are most likely to make major or legacy gifts. Give them the ability to grant you permission to engage with them and their trust in you will grow, their relationship with you will flourish, and their donations will increase.

## Convenience

Ours is a culture of convenience; we expect it in every area of our lives. Amazon.com is growing and profiting because it provides astounding levels of convenience to its customers. The same goes for iTunes and Facebook. Today, you can purchase a product, listen to music, or share information with your friends easier than ever.

News flash: Your donors are the same people who buy, download, and share. They not only want to gain value at a time of their choosing, they *expect* to be able to do so. Convenience is a powerful thing, and providing it greatly increases the chance that people will take the actions you desire.

Amazon, iTunes, and Facebook are always convenient, and if you want the value they provide, you know you can have it almost immediately. After all, what's more convenient than going online any time day or night, placing an order, then getting a big box with a smiley face on it? Amazon is ready to respond *at your convenience.* They are always working hard to figure out new ways to deliver timeliness, accessibility, and expedience.

At Amazon, and in the private sector, it's called customer service. It reduces friction and adds convenience. Unfortunately, there's not enough talk about *service* in the nonprofit sector. By the way, I prefer to call it "donor delight," but fundraisers seem to prefer words like *stewardship* or *donor relations.* Regardless, search for *customer service* online and you'll find information about what businesses do to support customer engagements and transactions. Search online for *donor service* and you'll find information about giving blood. Something is wrong here.

Still need more convincing? In the private sector, a study by Oracle Corporation titled "Managing Customer Effort" found that customer effort (which could otherwise be described as inconvenience) could be analyzed by developing feedback loops, collecting insights from customers, mapping out the engagement journey, and identifying friction points. According to the study, doing so helps businesses work to reduce friction along every step of the process during each engagement instance with a customer. When customer effort was reduced, Oracle found that customer satisfaction increased from 61 percent to 93 percent, customer loyalty increased from 69 percent to 87 percent, and willingness to recommend increased from 51 percent to 87 percent. Now just imagine if you could increase your organization's donor satisfaction, donor loyalty, and willingness to recommend similarly. Increase convenience and reduce friction, and you will.

So if you haven't gotten my point by now, you should aim to provide the same level of convenience as the private sector for three compelling reasons: 1) your donors expect it, 2) your donors deserve it, and 3) your competitors in the nonprofit sectors are reading this book, too!

# Test It

Are you now thinking about ways to deliver convenience and give donors what they want? I hope so. Why not start by looking at your website? If you're serious about providing convenience online, test your site's user experience by donating. Go ahead. Do it! See what it feels like to be a donor. Then answer these questions:

- Was it easy for you to give?

- How long did it take?

- Could you contact someone easily if you had trouble donating?

- Could you find a direct phone number or email for your Gift Officers online (so you could call or email them to discuss giving)?

- Could you click on that phone number or email using your mobile phone?

- Could you get a human being to talk to you about giving right now?

- Could you connect to a Gift Officer's LinkedIn profile directly from one of your web pages so you could check them out? Most donors will want to do that before meeting with a Gift Officer.

- How about giving from a donor-advised fund? Could you take that kind of action from your organization's site?

- Could you effortlessly provide feedback (perhaps in a survey)?

- Could you painlessly request information about programs or giving options?

- Could you sign up to volunteer?

- Could you opt in to get regular communications and updates? Or did they opt you in without your permission?

- Could you refer friends?

If you answered "no" to any of these questions, you'll want to work on your convenience factor so your supporters get the experience they deserve.

# Prompt Response

When a supporter finally decides they want to take some sort of action, you've got to be there for them. At the very least, respond quickly. Doing so will build their trust in you and your organization while proving that you truly care and are interested in satisfying their needs.

At MarketSmart, if you click our "Request A Demo" button during business hours to get a demonstration of our product suite, you can expect to get a response from us right away. Go ahead and try it! If you don't hear from someone promptly, let me know; my email is info@imarketsmart.com. If we respond quickly and provide you with convenience (as we should), let me know that, too. Either way, I'll send you a gift simply for providing me with feedback about my company's response times and the level of convenience we provide to you.

Clearly I care a lot about whether or not we respond promptly. That's because, like your nonprofit, I've invested exorbitant amounts of time and money to get people to my website so they eventually take action to seriously consider exchanging money for the value we provide. All of my investments in awareness building, interest building, and desire building would only be worthwhile if we respond promptly when people raise their hands (which is essentially what they do when they click our "Request A Demo" button). Prompt follow-up on leads is paramount. Lackadaisically responding to them would be like burning money, not to mention being just plain rude.

Sadly, follow-up failure is prevalent in every business category around the world. In 2011, the *Harvard Business Review* studied 2,241 U.S. companies to see how quickly they followed up on web-generated leads. What they found was alarming considering the astronomical amounts of resources that private-sector businesses spend on generating leads. Their data showed that:

- 37 percent responded within an hour

- 16 percent responded within 1–24 hours

- 24 percent took more than 24 hours

- 23 percent never responded at all[3]

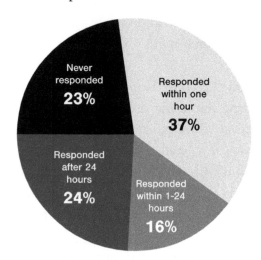

Source: Harvard Business Review study
titled "The Short Life of Online Sales Leads"

---

3   James B. Oldroyd, Kristina McElheran, and David Elkington, "The Short Life of Online Sales Leads," Harvard Business Review, last modified March 2011, accessed December 2, 2017, https://hbr.org/2011/03/the-short-life-of-online-sales-leads.

The *Harvard Business Review* found the results to be particularly shocking in light of a previous study in which they found the following:

> Firms that tried to contact potential customers within one hour of receiving an inquiry were nearly seven times as likely to qualify the lead (which was defined as having a meaningful conversation with a key decision maker) as those that tried to contact the customer even an hour later—and more than 60 times as likely as companies that wait 24 hours or longer.[4]

Could these figures hold true in the nonprofit sector, too? I think so. Clearly, responding to leads promptly provides delight to the very people who afford you a paycheck and support your mission. It's also simply the right thing to do.

# Leverage Technology to Respond Promptly

What if your shop is overworked, underpaid, and understaffed, like so many other nonprofits? How will you ever have the budget or staff to connect personally and conveniently with all your prospects? You don't have to. You can leverage technology to do it for you and come out ahead in both time and money.

After a supporter fills out a form online, they should get a relevant and personalized email letting them know the message was received. That same message might include an opportunity for the supporter to add details about their needs or arrange a call or meeting using an online calendar appointment-setting tool.

Just as technology can automate your responses to supporters online, it can also create two-way dialogue, build communities, connect people to one another on social media, and involve them so they'll participate in events or volunteer opportunities.

Embracing automation has become a necessity because donor expectations have changed. Donors don't necessarily want personal human contact right away.

4  Ibid.

Most of the time, it might actually be better to use technology to open two-way dialogue channels and give supporters something valuable they'll appreciate.

When you leverage technology to make a donor's engagements with your mission easy and effortless, you'll prove that you care about them. They'll thank you for your effort by giving more, exhibiting loyalty, and referring your nonprofit to like-minded friends and family members.

You don't need to invest in more staff to make convenience happen. By leveraging technology, one fundraiser can perform like a thousand. Embrace it. Then use it to deliver prompt responses that provide convenience and reduce effort. Your supporters deserve it!

# The Amazing Convenience Gizmo

For most donors, nothing is more convenient and accessible than the online channel—the internet—and its always-available, 24/7 nature. Even older donors use the internet. According to the Pew Research Center's 2017 survey of technology use among seniors, 67 percent of people over 65 are now online. Their adoption rate has taken off since 2000 when only 14 percent were using the channel. Plus, the more affluent and highly educated of the older users (your best donor prospects) are even more likely to be online. Ninety-two percent of college-educated seniors use the internet, as well as 94 percent of those with incomes greater than $75,000 per year.

Everyone agrees that the internet is a powerful gizmo that helps nonprofits engage with donors and prospective donors conveniently, on their schedule. Its ability to provide fundraisers with real-time data is unrivaled. Additionally, the digital nature of online engagement allows you to easily capture donor verbatims at low cost so you can understand why your supporters care, how they want to be treated, what they want to see, how they want to give, and more.

It gets better. The most experienced fundraisers have learned from countless face-to-face meetings with supporters that their nonverbal communications are often even more important than their spoken words. Their facial expressions, body posture, gestures, eye movements, voice intonations, and other actions help them understand what to say and when.

Digital body language works the same way. For instance, the person who clicked on the Donate Now button recently is a better prospect than the person who did it last year. The person who downloaded bequest language and forwarded it to an advisor last night is a better prospect than someone simply watching a video that same evening. And the person who sought information about giving from their donor-advised fund a moment ago is a better prospect than the one who hasn't engaged at all for weeks.

Just like poker players looking for "tells," you should look at your supporters' digital body language. By using technology that monitors and tracks each donor's digital body language online, you can determine when some of them might be much more likely to appreciate your outreach via telephone or email to set up a meeting, have a conversation, or ask for a donation.

Wouldn't you agree that the person clicking on the Donate Now button might deserve a relevant online experience in the same way that my family deserved an enhanced experience after waiting in long lines at Disney World on a hot summer day? Perhaps the person who abandons their donation cart might need a certain type of offer that involves them in a different way. Maybe they weren't ready to give because something was missing. What could it be? Find out quickly while they're online, respond instantly, and you might reduce their effort in a way that ensures they give.

Digital body language can also trigger highly relevant, personalized, contextual online experiences that satisfy donor needs right away. How convenient!

For instance, engagement fundraisers use exit surveys to capture vital information about why people abandon the donating process and bounce from their donation pages without making a gift. They also use sophisticated survey platforms like MarketSmart's immediately after the donation process is completed

# Convenience in Action: Retargeting Ads

Thanks to technology, the number of ways you can provide convenience for your supporters is never ending.

Consider a supporter clicking on "Make a Legacy Gift in Your Will" online. Soon after leaving your website, he would likely gain value from an online ad (or an email) that provides an opportunity for him to download a short report describing "Seven Tips for Creating a Will." Perhaps he might appreciate an offer for a video that explains how to leave more money to his family members and favorite charities in his will by using wise tax-planning strategies.

He could be made aware of these offers (the report or the video) thanks to highly appropriate and relevant retargeting ads that any nonprofit can serve up to the right people at the right times. They can be triggered to appear for him as he surfs the web and visits any sites that display ads to their visitors. You've probably noticed retargeting ads. They seem to follow you around.

If they're appropriate and used sparingly, they'll be effective because they'll ensure that your donors get relevant offers (ads) online after they leave your pages and visit ESPN, USA Today, or any other site online that is part of the Google Advertising Network.

Here's how it works: A simple, tiny line of code is placed on the page (i.e., the "Make a Legacy Gift in Your Will" page). The code drops a cookie on the web surfer's browser signaling to Google what ad to serve up as the donor visits other sites online. The donor is going to get ads on those sites anyway. Why not ensure the ads provide relevant and valuable offers for engagement back on your pages instead of the usual random automobile ads?

Retargeting is powerful, it works, and it's very cost-effective because it gives the right messages to the right people. Unlike direct mail, it's very nimble. You can control how often the ads appear and you can monitor the results metrics closely to test what works so you can optimize your budget relatively quickly. In addition, you can pay for the advertising based on impressions or clicks and stop the campaign at will. I recommend trying several ads to see which work best.

For the supporter clicking on Make a Legacy Gift in Your Will online, a retargeting ad that offers a relevant report or video might be just what he needed. Offering those items to her later, sparingly, would be convenient. Don't you agree?

online. By doing so, they do much more than just supply their supporters with a tax receipt. They give their supporters a chance to provide feedback, tell why they care about the cause, describe their interests, and answer valuable donor profile questions like whether they have already made a legacy gift (for instance).

If the donor answers "yes" (a verbatim) regarding the legacy gift, they might instantly see an online page that provides them with an opportunity to explain how they want their generous gift to be used, what programs they want to support, whether they want their gift to be restricted, whether it was made to commemorate or honor someone in particular, etc. Get the picture?

If the fundraiser arms himself with relevant information and permission to use it, he can develop proper stewardship offers that will resonate with that particular donor. Every stewardship touch going forward will be exponentially more beneficial to the donor, thereby ensuring that the gift will remain in their estate plan and perhaps even increase in size.

The amazing convenience gizmo is here to stay. Use it to your advantage and leverage it to help you raise more money, faster, and at lower cost.

# Relevance and Value

Think about this scenario: You're working under a tight deadline at your desk, and Joe from accounting comes into your office to say hello. You aren't sure why he's there, and it's annoying. You don't really know Joe, and you have nothing in common with him. He doesn't even work in your department. You're thinking, *Why are you even here? Go back to your cubicle. Leave me alone. I'm busy.* Then he asks you to help him with a problem he's having with his wife. You say, "No." The entire encounter is awkward and unfulfilling. Exasperated, you go back to the task at hand.

Now consider this: You're working under a tight deadline at your desk and Julie comes into your office to say hello. You know Julie. In the past, you've talked about the fact that you both have kids around the same ages and she works in your department. She heard through the grapevine that you were working on something for which she could provide assistance. She offers up a solution you hadn't envisioned. It's a great idea that will save you hours of work and free you from frustration. After you chat with Julie for a few minutes, you feel grateful for her visit. Then you go back to the task at hand, happy in your new knowledge.

What's the difference? Clearly, being interrupted by someone who's irrelevant to your situation and only wants to take something from you is more annoying than being interrupted by someone who's highly relevant and wants to help you. We don't like intrusions, but we're much more accepting of them when they're relevant and we're gaining value from them.

Fundraisers no longer have to interrupt people at the wrong times with irrelevant communications. Nonprofits that listen effectively to donor verbatims and digital body language can be relevant and provide value to their supporters. When they do, it's not an interruption at all. It's engagement, and it's welcomed.

You want your organization to be like an old friend or family member whom the donor can depend on. You might ask them for money every once in a while, but you've consistently engaged with them, so they already know about the problem. The donor has been involved from the beginning and they know that you really need the money and that it will be put to good use. They know you aren't going to hit them up all the time, or sell their name to another charity. You share a level of trust and belief in the mission, so the donor welcomes the opportunity to give.

## Anonymity and Assistance

Before or after giving, some donors want to be anonymous. Their preference may be based in religion or personality, or simply because they don't care about notoriety. Many donors prefer anonymity because they're fearful of getting inundated with requests for donations from other charities. Regardless of the reasons, a donor's request for anonymity has to be respected.

During the consideration process, some donors seek anonymity because they aren't ready to reveal who they are—at least not yet. They're checking you out. They're conducting research. I once knew a wealthy woman who volunteered as a docent at a museum, not only to get more involved, but also to determine whether or not they were worthy of her money. She was doing what any wise investor might do. Can you blame her for being cautious?

Engagement fundraisers don't make "moves"; they allow donors to navigate the process on their own. They let them qualify themselves, educate themselves, involve themselves, and, more and more often, solicit themselves. I call these the "four selfs" of Engagement Fundraising. It's okay to let donors do all of them anonymously until their trust is developed and they're ready to talk to or meet with someone.

**The "Four Selfs" of Engagement Fundraising.**

Giving the donor space doesn't mean you should remove yourself from the process entirely. Just be cognizant of the fact that most donors want to contemplate how to find meaning in their lives on their own. Don't worry. Most will still welcome your help to keep the ball rolling. They just won't want you coming by their office interrupting them with irrelevant, valueless interruptions like Joe from accounting.

Engagement fundraisers recognize there will always be window-shoppers and tire kickers out there. The trick is to leverage technology in a way that lets them look around, test you out at their own pace, and involve themselves as they want. Don't force things. Help support their decision making, and recognize when they're ready and the time is right for you to jump in.

Hounding a donor for attention or action before they're ready will only annoy them and burn your bridges. Providing value and relevance while allowing them to be anonymous will make them feel respected and grow their trust in you and your organization.

Some fundraisers can't help themselves. They have to be the star of the show. They have to talk. They don't want to give their supporters the space they need. They don't want to listen. I call these people *show up and throw up fundraisers*. They're annoying and they find themselves changing jobs every couple of years until they finally leave the profession altogether. They never learn a valuable lesson I was taught back in college.

I was working for the school newspaper, *The Diamondback*. I had a great meeting with the owner of a local pizza shop. We collaborated on a great offer: buy one large pizza, get one free. I sketched an ad and handed him my drawing. He was pretty happy with the concept. I'd done everything right. He was interested and had built up a level of desire for buying the ad. So I went in for the close. As I handed him a pen to sign the contract I asked, "So should we go forward with this?"

He became quiet. He sat there staring at my ad for what seemed like an eternity. That's when I screwed it all up. I failed to let him have the consideration time he needed. The silence was too much for me; I couldn't help myself and I started blurting out a lot of facts, figures, and reasons why he should do it. He was polite. He listened.

So I continued with anecdotes and stories about my friends. I assured him that this was the kind of deal they'd want. He listened.

I babbled on like an idiot. He listened.

When he tried to speak I even interrupted him.

Then, when he finally got a chance to speak, he harshly said, "Don't they teach you anything about how to close a deal in college? I was thinking! Now get out of my shop!!"

I'd blown it. He was silent and I couldn't handle it. I made it all about me. I couldn't get past myself and let him come to a decision on his own. I was too engrossed in myself to allow him the time to do what he needed to do as he considered his decision. He had a process, it was his process, and I wasn't going to change that. I needed to let him go through it on his own.

# Technology—The Agent of Change

Technology is the great equalizer, the agent of change. It enables disruption, and it's powerful. The question is: What are you doing about it? Is technology your friend?

If you don't want to embrace it and reap the benefits, you'll have to deal with the fact that your competitors probably are. History shows us that technology has disrupted seemingly untouchable industries as shown by the following instructive tales.

## Transportation and Taxis

Have you ever said, "Hey, I'd really like to take a taxi because it's such an immensely enjoyable experience"? Don't answer. I know what you'd say. No one truly enjoys a taxi ride.

It starts when you call a cab company and get a rude individual on the phone who probably lies to you about how short a time it will be until the taxi shows up. You're really not sure the cab will show at all, but you go for it. Then you stand and wait. And wait. The taxi shows up, and the air conditioner doesn't work. It's 92 degrees and very humid. The windows are down, for which you're grateful. The driver is smoking a cigarette. You'll deal with smelling like smoke and looking disheveled and windblown later. Sometimes the driver is in too much of a hurry and drives out of control, because he thinks you want to get there fast. In actuality, you'd really just like to get there alive. You get out of the taxi and pay. The driver is mad, because he thinks you didn't tip him enough.

Enter Uber. When I first heard of Uber, I was with a friend who suggested we "grab an Uber." He told me it was good, and I'd love it, because "everyone loves Uber." I got the app. I could see where the car was when I called it, and I knew exactly when it would arrive. If there was an issue, I could call or text the driver, or he could call or text me. The driver was nice and cheerful. The car was clean. There was a bottle of water and a mint. It was a safe ride with air conditioning. I felt confident I would arrive safely, and I did. I was tied to the experience through ratings, and I could use the feedback loop so the driver and company could improve. They never asked for a tip. Everything was transparent, comforting, and easy.

Thanks to technology, the entire taxicab industry has run into competition it could never have foreseen, and it's been changed forever.

## Encyclopedias

When I was a kid, encyclopedia salesmen would visit people in their homes to sell their books. The process started with an interruption by the telemarketing team that set the appointments by mentioning that our neighbors had accepted a visit and the representative would only be in the area for a short while. Then the salesperson would visit right on time. The presentation was artful and slick. It began with a list of the neighbors who already bought the set. Then it continued using a powerful strategy called "the four walls technique" that relies on every human being's desire to remain consistent. The salesman would skillfully ask four questions to which he was sure the customer would answer yes, thereby "boxing in" the customer so they felt pressure that resulted in a decision to buy.

The questions would follow a preconceived outline, such as:

First question (wall): Do you think education is important for your children?

Second question (wall): Do you think a child who does their homework well would be more likely to get a good education?

Third question (wall): Wouldn't you agree that a child who has a good set of reference books would be likely to do their homework well?

Fourth final question (box): Then it sounds like you really would benefit from our encyclopedias, right?

Sure, it was manipulative. But my parents and all the others in the neighborhood bought the books. Then they sat on the shelf in the den 99.99 percent of the time, as a frequent reminder of how much money they'd wasted. Of course they couldn't throw them away just because they had a bad sales experience. Instead, they hoped that maybe the kids would use them every once in a while (even though they could have gone to the library).

For a long time thereafter, I'm sure they felt annoyed because they were pressured and shamed into buying something they didn't really need or want. When my mom passed away 30 years later, I was confronted with what to do with the pile of books. As I pondered that dilemma, I also thought about how technology brought change to the encyclopedia industry. Instead of there being only a small group of authors or books explaining the world, an ever-growing and always-changing organism was built by the collective force of humanity, checked and reviewed for accuracy by others, with no money changing hands. It was called Wikipedia.

Wikipedia writers don't share information with the world because they were hired to do it. They do it because they believe in the concept of getting it right and making information available for everyone. They do it for free in a collaborative spirit for the forces of good.

Now anyone with an internet connection can tap into that brilliance and interconnect from story to story, or information point to information point, and delve deeper and wider into any subject they choose. It's convenient and essentially free (as long as you have a device to tap into it).

In the 1990s, technology swept in like a fresh breeze ushering in the end of an era that began in 1768, when *Encyclopedia Britannica* was first published. By 1996, the company had laid off every single salesperson after milking its persuasive (or manipulative) tactics for 60 years. The print version of the books stuck around a little longer before it was terminated in 2012 as the company transitioned to the digital world. Now, thanks to a strategy that embraced disruptive innovation and a renewed focus on their value proposition, the company is profitably selling mostly to schools and universities.

### Ready or Not

These case studies refer to industries that were thought to be impervious to change. Their own refusal to evolve in the face of technological advances ultimately changed the way business was conducted—to their detriment.

Fundraisers take note. It's time to turn away from orthodoxies and stop listening in echo chambers filled with misdirection and misinformation. Technology is a disruptor, but that doesn't mean disaster. It's actually an opportunity. You can leverage innovations to give your donors what they deserve, so they'll end up giving more.

Each donor also has their own process for making their decisions. Chances are you don't know what that is, so the best move is no move at all, especially if their process involves anonymity.

Let them think until they're ready. Listen. Look for cues. Then make sure you're there for them when they want you to facilitate the giving process. Don't force it by interrupting them with irrelevant spam, junk mail, telemarketing, or blurting out facts and figures in person. Trying to "move," convince, cajole, or manipulate them will get you nowhere. If you're not a helpful part of the process, you'll get thrown out of it altogether.

# A New Job Title

In the face of technology and new donor expectations, the core job of the fundraiser actually hasn't changed much at all. Your task has always been about facilitating giving and connecting the following dots:

- The mission of the organization

- The programs that need funding

- How the mission entwines with a donor's story

- How giving can make someone feel good about being the hero in their story, an advocate for change, a righter of wrongs, etc.

Every mission is not right for every donor. A mission is right only for the donor with a personal connection to it. Your challenge is to collect verbatims and digital body language, and then help connect it all. Connection happens when you engage with people in a convenient way that provides value through offers for engagement and involvement. More importantly, the offers should make people feel good, know that they've been heard, and believe that they're part of something bigger than themselves.

Leave your own tales at the door, and focus on the donor's story. Most of us make the mistake of talking way too much when we should be *listening*. It's the only way to discover donor needs and desires and align them with your organization.

Sometimes the more things change, the more they stay the same. Even with all the technology available to you, your aim should still be to meet donor expectations. To be an *engagement facilitator*.

Wouldn't you rather be a facilitator than a "fundraiser"? You may not want to acknowledge it, but "fundraiser" screams "salesperson" to many donors. It makes a lot of people want to hide their wallet. In contrast, a facilitator is helpful, ready to answer questions, and able to make the process of giving as seamless and easy as possible. Could it be that a facilitator helps donors meet *their* needs while a fundraiser helps meet the needs of the organization?

Turns out, what you call yourself actually can make a difference. Dr. Russell James, J.D., Ph.D., CFP®, researched what fundraiser job titles inspire more engagement, connectivity, and giving among donors.

As a professor at Texas Tech University where he directs the on-campus and on-line graduate program in Charitable Financial Planning, as well as Charitable Gift Law at the Texas Tech University School of Law, Dr. James also researches brain activity in fundraising prospects. According to Dr. James, his study tested "the impact of various fundraiser job titles on others' willingness to contact the fundraiser to engage in giving related discussions."[5]

First, he determined that fundraiser job titles tend to fall into one of three categories: institution-focused, gift-focused, or donor-focused. The donor-focused titles tended to perform better than the others. Interestingly, after testing 63 titles, he found it was a challenge to provide a title to the research participants that seriously made donors want to contact a fundraiser or engage in discussions about giving.

---

5 Russell N. James III, "Testing the Effectiveness of Fundraiser Job Titles in Charitable Bequest and Complex Gift Planning," *Nonprofit Management & Leadership* 27, no. 2 (Winter 2016), page 166.

Some of the titles he tested included Director or Vice President of:

- Institutional Advancement

- Charitable Estate Planning

- Real Estate Gifting

- Gift Planning

- Estate & Gift Planning

- Planned Giving & Estate Administration

- Trusts, Estates & Gift Planning

- Charitable Estate Planning

- Trusts & Estates

- Donor Relations

- Advancement

- Development & Marketing

- Institutional Advancement (surely the worst of the bunch)

- Development

- Advancement Development

- Business Development

- Executive

- External Relations

- Donor Ombudsman

I wasn't surprised by the results. I've always found these kinds of titles to be off-putting. They don't reflect what donors want and what the best fundraisers actually do. Great fundraisers are facilitators, donor-centric representatives who discover donor motives and provide value without expecting anything in return. Try a new title and see if your mindset changes for the better.

Need more proof? If you can think of yourself in terms of being a facilitator, you'll be less anxious about approaching donors and asking for money. The anxiety disappears, because facilitators don't ask. They provide supporters with opportunities to change the world and they help them make an impact.

# There is hope

Although what donors want has changed, communication channels have transformed, and competition for donor dollars is greater than ever—there's hope. It's true that the charitable sector is growing, but most charitable organizations refuse to evolve. This presents a golden opportunity for those willing to change.

Organizations that engage their donors and evolve with technological advancements will stand out. Supporters are thirsty for engagement. When you quench that thirst, donations follow.

Try to understand individual donor motivations. Move away from the short-term results of the latest email blast, event, or direct mail drop, and focus on building relationships and offering engagement experiences.

Fundraising strategies that work don't happen overnight. They have to incorporate a degree of patience. As with fishing, you catch more if you fish where the fish are and can wait until the fish fully take the bait, instead of yanking the line at the first nibble.

Be a facilitator; let the bait sit. Give before you try to get. Provide value. Offer opportunities for people to better themselves. Keep a donor-centric, donor-delight, facilitation-oriented mindset, and you will meet your goals.

# Part Two
# Engagement Fundraising

# Chapter 3
# Why Donors Give

Do you know the number-one reason people give? It's not what you think.

The main reason people give is because they want to feel good. Imagine a donor seeing a picture of villagers drinking clean water from a well that she helped finance. Of course, she's happy that she helped better the lives of others, but something is happening on a more physical level. She's literally flooded by pleasurable physical sensations as endorphins are released. This "warm glow" created by the dopamine hit feels good, and the giver wants more of that feeling. "Feeling good" becomes a habit.

Research supports the idea that giving makes us happy. In studies using MRIs, the pleasure and reward area of the midbrain lights up when people give to a charity. It's the same part of the brain associated with the good feelings surrounding love. When people give, their stress is lowered, and they feel more connected.

Re-creating the "warm glow" for donors is what Engagement Fundraising is all about and why it works so well. Although the biological response is the goal that keeps donors seeking the next hit of dopamine and oxytocin, there are a number of nuanced motivators that initially engage them.

New technologies can help you identify all the motivating factors behind giving and help you engage your donors more effectively by targeting your offers and appeals accordingly. These same innovations deliver convenience and engage potential donors faster. Donors want immediate satisfaction and immediate rewards. Using Engagement Fundraising, you can give them what they want better than ever before.

# Common Motivators

Your goal as a facilitator is to understand what's motivating a donor in order to connect the dots. Donors are motivated to give, whether they know it or not. If you can use the prospect's verbatims and read their digital body language, you can pinpoint how that donor wants to realize their philanthropic goals. Then you can *facilitate* the process.

Motivators that pop up often include:

- **Recognition:** A donor gives because they want the fame or notoriety of being charitable in a certain way. For example, the donor gives to an arts center so that the new auditorium is named for her, or so there's a brick with her name on it, or so he gets to see his name in the concert series program.

- **Social consequence:** A donor gives because they're seeking status within their community or particular social circles. For example, the donor may want to be associated with certain cultural events in her city.

- **Family legacy:** New generations of donors give in certain ways because it's part of their family history and reputation. Perhaps the donor's family has always been patrons of the arts or champions of the poor. For example, being born a Carnegie might mean she's part of a dynasty, and it's expected she'll be charitable.

- **Eternal reward:** This donor is worried that future generations will view him poorly, or he may be worried how he will be judged in the afterlife. Ebenezer Scrooge understood from his dream that he would die unliked and unloved, that he would always be remembered as an uncharitable miser. So he changed.

- **Taxes Incentives:** Some donors try to save themselves money. They will give to charities in order to lower their tax bracket or ensure their heirs pay less inheritance tax.

- **Transactional:** A donor may give in order to receive certain perks. For example, she may give $50,000 to the university and in return get a good parking spot and a place in the president's suite for football games.

- **Advocacy:** The donor may want to right specific wrongs or lobby for a particular cause. For example, he might give to organizations that align with his political beliefs and fight on his behalf.

- **Personal obligation:** Donors may want to repay an institution that helped them in the past. For example, a successful entrepreneur might donate regularly to her old business school to express gratitude for her scholarship.

- **Community:** A donor may want to help his own community or help foster a sense of community in an area that's important to him. For example, LeBron James is very philanthropic in his hometown of Cleveland.

- **To set an example:** A donor may give in order to encourage other donations. For example, Bill Gates and Warren Buffett made a giving pledge in the hope that other wealthy people would follow.

- **Investment:** A donor may give in order to make the world better. For example, a donor might fund scholarships, or build a road, because she knows that the investment will pay off in ways greater than a personal benefit.

There are other motivators, but these are the most common, and it's rare that a donor is moved to give by only one. The point of understanding what motivates a donation is so that you can use Engagement Fundraising techniques to address the motivation and meet the need of that donor.

Some people disagree that there's always a motivator at work; they claim it's possible for giving to be purely altruistic. I disagree. The only way giving could be purely altruistic is if the donor had no idea that their money was donated. If the giver knows about the gift, which she does, she's going to have some feeling about it that probably fits into one of the motivators just listed. Even if the donor simply likes feeling that she's a good, moral person, the giving is satisfying a need to see herself in that way.

But that's okay. Regardless of the motivator, the value in giving isn't diminished.

# A Valuable Exchange

We've already made it clear that one of the keys to Engagement Fundraising is the 80/20 rule, the Pareto principle. It pays (literally) to focus on the 20 percent of the people who make up 80 percent of an organization's donations. Although the motivators just discussed are general to all donors, you have to go a little deeper to connect with your 20 percent and cultivate major donations and legacy gifts.

First, you need to know where to look. The data shows there's a sweet spot for giving. The older people get, the more they give, but at a certain point, they're done. Baby boomers are the primary givers to charity at this time. Younger generations are just trying to survive, and a growing number of those older than the baby boomers have already made their plans.

It makes sense. When you're 26 years old, you're not reflecting on much. You may want to do good and have a meaningful life, but you don't have the money to give much yet, and you know you've got your whole life ahead of you to donate. At the other end of the spectrum, older people have already made peace with their reputation and made their plans, and may not even be managing their own money anymore.

Once you find your 20 percent, you have to facilitate an exchange—their money for some value, or perceived value, in the charity. How is this value determined? What can your nonprofit provide to the charitably-minded person? There are four of them, and the high-level value is the easiest: help the supporter *feel good*. It's the main reason people give.

The next value that a nonprofit can provide is *autobiographical heroism*, helping donors see themselves as the hero in their own life story. Everyone wants to be the good guy. If you can help a supporter recount their life and see how it entwines with your mission, they'll get it. Their opportunity to gain personal heroism will become apparent. In fact, did you ever wonder about the primary difference between for-profit marketing and nonprofit fundraising? In the private sector, successful for-profit marketers often make their product or service the hero. In the nonprofit sector, successful fundraisers make their donors the heroes not their organizations.

Imagine that someone is grateful to the hospital and the volunteers that helped her mother when she had cancer. A facilitator's goal is to gently help the donor visualize and recount what a hard time it was, how wonderful her mother had been taken care of, and how kind the staff had been during such a difficult time. She'll be motivated to give to the hospital because she wants to be the hero in the story making sure others get a chance to benefit from the staff too.

*Symbolic immortality* is a third value that resonates with prospects. It's more than letting the supporter be a hero in her own life story; it's helping her realize that she can live on in the minds of others. Symbolic immortality is the reason stars make a contribution of around $30,000 to have their names on the "Walk of Fame" in Hollywood, and it's why people give to have their names on buildings at colleges and universities.

One valuable engagement offer that MarketSmart provides to people on behalf of a charity client includes a workbook to help them create a memoir. Everyone can't afford a building with their name on it, but the memoir workbook is a valuable offer, because it helps people pass down their stories and life lessons. Once they complete the project, they achieve symbolic immortality.

A final value you can provide to supporters is *commemorative immortality*. You give a donor an opportunity to honor someone. The donor may be willing to trade money for the chance to run a race in honor of her grandmother, or to donate in honor of a great aunt. Interestingly, Dr. Russell James's research shows that the honoree is usually a female relative (mother, grandmother, etc.).

# Laws of Influence

So far, we've discussed ways of influencing donors by connecting and engaging around their particular common motivators (recognition, family legacy, taxes, etc.), ways of creating value (autobiographical heroism, commemorative immortality, etc.)—and by making them feel good!

There is another category of influencers from the book *Influence* by Robert B. Cialdini that should be added to the mix. Cialdini defines six universal laws of persuasion.

Remember, the best salespeople don't pressure. They're simply adept at helping others make decisions they really want to make. They know that everyone likes to buy but no one likes to be sold. Similarly, your supporters like to give but they don't like to be solicited. You can use the following laws of influence to understand the psychology of persuasion so everyone wins:

1. **Reciprocity:** This social convention makes supporters feel strongly that they have an obligation to repay when something is given to them. By using the law of reciprocity, you provide value to supporters first, knowing that your gifts will inspire them to want to return the favor in the future. You give so you get.

2. **Consistency:** This reflects our need for personal alignment. It's human nature to crave consistency and resist change. You can meet this need by keeping communications consistent, keeping the same look, and having the communication always come from the same person. Consistently providing value to your supporters over time builds a relationship of trust.

3. **Social proof:** People will get on the bandwagon once they see others like themselves on it, or that people want to be part of a donor community that includes famous or influential individuals, friends, or like-minded people.

4. **Liking:** People more easily persuade us if we like them or if we believe they like us.

5. **Authority:** People are more likely to pay attention to or follow someone they perceive as important or who's an authority figure. For example, before someone gives a major gift to a diabetes charity, they may need a researcher or doctor to explain how the money will be spent in the lab.

6. **Scarcity:** We always want what we can't have. Perceived scarcity generates demand and urgency. Deadlines and limited naming opportunities create scarcity.

These laws of influence have always been around. They aren't new. What's new is our way of using them to greater advantage in fundraising.

Don't be confused by all of these different motivators and influencers. They are simply arrows in your marketing quiver. Sometimes you'll be mixing the common motivators, the motivators for creating value, and Cialdini's universal laws of persuasion. You might use the universal law of scarcity in line with the value-creating desire for symbolic immortality and notoriety. For example, you might put a deadline of January 31st on a campaign for naming a building.

You've created an opportunity for symbolic immortality and notoriety, but the opportunity is fleeting. It ends if donors don't act fast.

Before technology changed things, the world of major gift and legacy fundraising was quite different. You might have had a list, some three-by-five cards, a pen, and a phone. You would meet with every donor individually and conduct a donor discovery visit. You would build a relationship with the donor, and the two of you would get to know each other. You might bring a little gift, hoping to invoke the law of reciprocity. You would always wear a suit to show that you were an authority and a capable individual. This was all done one donor at a time. There was a lot of information that had to be sorted and analyzed and recorded. It was extremely time-consuming and extremely slow.

Compare that to Engagement Fundraising today. You can reach out to hundreds or hundreds of thousands of supporters by conducting donor discovery digitally or through direct mail. If you're using the right technologies, the computer can start prioritizing them by sorting where people are in the consideration process, why they care, what their needs and desires are, and what offers motivate them to engage. Then you can facilitate the giving experience and deliver donor delight by using the laws of influence to gently build trust and encourage people to do what they already want to do: give so they feel good.

# Chapter 4
# Stages and Strategies

I ran into a Major Gift Officer at a fundraising conference who worked for the university where I'd attended journalism school. He invited me to get together for coffee the following week to fill me in on what was happening on campus.

Of course, he didn't realize my office is so close to the school that I can see the football stadium from my desk. My father-in-law also worked there as the Comptroller during that period, so I got filled in all the time. Furthermore, I go to the football and basketball games. I even frequently eat lunch on campus as I read the school newspaper. I didn't say this, but I probably knew more about what was going on at the university than he did.

I told him a meeting wasn't necessary and I explained why. He replied, "Well, what do you think about giving? Want to make a donation?"

Do I even need to tell you my answer?

My refusal to give at the time had nothing to do with him personally, but I got nothing from him at the time and didn't see much reason to build a relationship. He provided no value and he moved too fast. He knew nothing about me, so his ask fell flat.

Would anything have caused me to write a check that day? Would anything have caused me to write a check later on? Maybe.

Perhaps if he knew which school I'd graduated from and how that related to my career, or that I loved going to the basketball games, I would have been more interested. What if he said, "Hey, there's going to be a meet-up for grads of the College of Journalism before the basketball game and we've got tickets for anyone that wants to go afterward. You don't have to sit with me, but you'll get to mingle with other alumni and maybe make some new contacts." I would've been all in!

Imagine if, after that first event and over a period of time, he learned about my story, how I started my business, how my college education impacted my life, and how I'm currently engaged with the university. Imagine if he learned that I actually bought two of the old seats and part of the wooden floor from Cole Field House, the original basketball arena that opened in the 1950s and closed in 2002 soon after the Maryland Terrapins men's team won the national championship. Imagine if he learned that I got a basketball signed by Juan Dixon that year, the MVP of the final game. Imagine if he learned that I actually help one of the schools at the university raise money by providing them with free software and services. Plus, my office is crawling with energetic interns studying at the university and employees who graduated from there.

If he were patient, attentive, and inquisitive, would he have been able to provide me with more value by aligning opportunities to get involved or donate with my current life, my life story, where I resided in the consideration process, and my desire to find meaning in my life by helping others? Yes.

After providing me with value, would he have been able to ask me to give to support something that fit my needs? Yes.

Would his ask have been successful? Yes.

This story highlights the importance of understanding someone's life experiences and where someone resides in the consideration process. When you know what stage they're in, you can develop offers that will resonate with supporters so they'll move themselves toward a mutually beneficial decision.

# The Donor Journey

Rarely is the making of a major gift or a legacy gift done entirely on impulse. It's often a *highly considered decision* that takes time because it involves powerful emotions, thoughtful investigation, and discussions with influencers and advisors. In the private sector, highly considered sales involve a *consideration process*. In the nonprofit sector, I like to call it the *donor journey*.

The donor journey can happen over a relatively short period or become drawn out over decades. For some gifts, especially legacy gifts, the journey only ends when the donor passes away. Before that time finally comes, donors' lives change and their interests evolve. The likelihood that a donor will make a gift rises and falls over time. How you treat your donors when they aren't face-to-face with you, as they experience the donor journey, will ultimately make the difference in terms of whether they give during their lifetime and make room for you in their will.

Engaging with your donors is not a one-size-fits-all method. Every donor is unique and will require different things. Imagine plotting out each donor's individuality using a humongous version of a Rubik's Cube. As you probably know, the Rubik's Cube is a solid cube made up of smaller cubes that can be twisted and turned without falling apart. Each side has different colors that become scrambled once they're contorted. The standard Rubik's Cube has 54 individual cubes that make six colored sides when they're perfectly ordered, but can be mixed up to make over 43 quintillion potential configurations (43,252,003,274,489,856,000). In fact, if you were to turn a Rubik's Cube once every second to make a new pattern, it would take you trillions of years to see all the possibilities.

Now think about the individualities of your donors. Every single donor is as unique as a mixed-up Rubik's Cube.

If that isn't daunting enough, recognize that each donor's colors surely get re-arranged over time. Their relationship with your organization and its mission will fluctuate. They'll become involved and uninvolved. They'll care more and they'll care less. They'll read some emails or letters and they'll ignore others.

World-renowned fundraiser and author of the Clairification blog, Claire Axelrad, likens the donor journey to a vortex—an energized circle—saying, "At times some folks have more energy than others. People move in and out of the circle, giving and getting, as the time and spirit moves them."

With this complex image in mind, I hope you'll give your fundraising team a pat on the back. Cracking the code for each donor is challenging with the right technologies and support, and can be impossible without them.

# The Consideration Continuum

People are fickle. One day they love your charity. The next day they don't. On other days they're somewhere in between. They're busy. They get distracted. Their emotions run hot and cold.

With so many for-profits and other nonprofit suitors competing for your supporters' share of wallet, your supporters will always be wondering in the back of their minds, "What have you done for me lately?" If your answer is simply, "Give us money again!," you might have a problem.

One day I was working on a client project with Phyllis Freedman, one of the best legacy gift marketing experts I've ever known. She commented that the fickle nature of donor-charity relationships results in a "consideration continuum." That's because supporters' needs and interests are fluid. Major life events affect their interests, perceptions, and decisions. If you aren't engaging them, listening to understand their needs, and providing them with highly relevant and personalized value, another charity will.

I like to turn the original four-step funnel on its side to visualize the consideration continuum in the context of Engagement Fundraising and the donor journey. Doing so makes it easy to envision how a supporter might move forward and backward. This helps make it clear that loyalty is not a given. Even after a donation has been made, you can't stop being awesome. You can't stop providing outstanding service. And, you can't stop tracking tidbits of information about your supporters' online and offline wants, needs, and interests so you can continue to understand who they are, why they care, and what motivates them as their lives change.

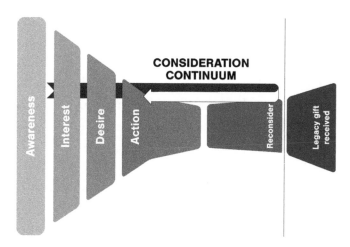

**The original four-step funnel and the consideration continuum.**

The first step along the continuum is *awareness*. In a traditional funnel, it's the top or the widest part of the funnel. At this stage, you're simply trying to build awareness around a certain problem, objective, offer, or opportunity.

Awareness can be built on several levels. There is high-level awareness, regarding the mission of an organization—perhaps bringing attention to the fact that there are children in need in a certain country. With Engagement Fundraising, however, you might be focused on generating awareness among people with capacity, or who are involved and may or may not have given in the past. Or, you could aim to build awareness for a certain project (like construction of a new building) or a type of gift option (such as a charitable gift annuity).

The second step is *interest*. Once someone is aware, you want them to lean in a bit and take a small action. That might be a simple click on an email, a view of a video, or a download. But it also could be a call to you, an opt-in to your e-newsletter, or registration for volunteering opportunities. Interest-stage engagements indicate that your supporter is beginning to understand the value a relationship with your organization can bring into their life.

Next, you'll want to help them turn their interest into *desire* so they eventually take action. At the desire step, your supporter must be engaged persistently, yet sensitively, with valuable, highly relevant, and personalized communications that align as perfectly as possible with their needs.

If you've done a great job helping your supporters understand how they can benefit from taking action, they will. If they're hung up at one stage of the consideration continuum or going backward in the process, it could be because you failed to make them feel good. Perhaps you haven't:

- **Built credibility.** Your supporters must feel good knowing they won't be wasting their time, effort, and hard-earned cash. They'll want assurance that they can trust in your organization and its leaders to help them accomplish their goals based on their reasons for giving.

- **Shown capability.** They must feel confident that your organization can do the job. Prove to them that your staff, equipment, and infrastructure are ready to make good on the organization's promises.

- **Fostered donor involvement.** They must feel like they're part of the team and that joining forces ensures that everyone will win. Helping them involve themselves in the problem and showing them how they can be part of the solution is essential.

- **Focused on their connection.** Their life story and personal mission must be entwined with the organization in a way that calls them to action.

- **Delivered value.** If you haven't listened enough to learn about them as people (not targets), understood their interests, or shown you care about them, they'll feel unappreciated and mistreated and will search for an organization that will better attend to their needs.

Once they take action, your job is not finished. In fact, in many respects, it's just begun. The minute the money leaves your supporters' bank accounts, they'll start to reevaluate you and your organization. They'll ask themselves, "What did they do with my money?" Then they'll reconsider your credibility and capability, they'll wonder if they should remain involved, and they'll weigh the amount of value they received.

Engagement Fundraising is a marathon, not a sprint. It's about delivering donor delight, not donor remorse.

## Sharon's Donor Journey

Imagine Sharon, age 74, has been a loyal donor to your hospital for 11 years. Her husband had cancer and passed away, but she'll never forget the support she received from your hospital and its staff. Yet, she's never considered a legacy gift. Although she received a fairly large benefit from her husband's life insurance policy and she has no debt, she hasn't thought much about where her money will go after her lifetime. By the way, Sharon has no children.

One day after "liking" her friend's photos on Facebook, Sharon comes across the opportunity to take a survey. For your organization, it's a *lead generation* campaign aimed to get her into the Engagement Fundraising vortex. Since her life story involves the hospital, she clicks the button to provide her feedback. When she gets to the seventh question, she learns she can help future generations by making a legacy gift—a concept she hadn't previously considered. Then, to answer a question in the survey, she lets you and the hospital know that she "might consider" making that kind of gift someday. She is now *aware* of that option and has shown some *interest* in it. But after she finishes taking the survey and hits Submit, she moves on to other things.

Weeks go by and one morning Sharon receives a personalized and highly relevant email. The email gives her an opportunity to see testimonials and videos, including stories of others like her who have beautiful stories and inspiring reasons to make a legacy gift to the hospital, too. She involves herself with those videos and browses through the stories about those others who found meaning in their lives as a result of making a legacy gift.

One story in particular caught her attention. Melvin, age 82, tells how he discovered he could leave his home to the hospital after his lifetime. Her *interest* in such a gift grows, but she goes back to her other email before going out to do errands.

Several weeks pass. As Sharon comes home from grocery shopping, she brings in her mail to find a hand-addressed letter. When she opens it, she learns how she can leave her home to the hospital while living in it until the end of her life. In addition, she can receive an income from that commitment as well as a nice tax write-off. The letter is simple, personal, warm, and friendly. In fact, it's signed by you!

The letter and its offer make sense to Sharon since she doesn't have any children. She loves her home and never wants to leave it. After all, that's where she lived with her husband for decades. Now, thanks to your highly relevant and personalized outreach, her *desire* to make a legacy gift begins to grow. She understands the value she can gain from the exchange that, of course, includes the good feelings she can attain knowing she's helping the hospital that helped her so much in her time of need. She doesn't respond to the letter. Instead she puts it aside in a drawer she keeps for these sorts of things.

Months go by. From time to time she reads letters and clicks on emails from you. After a visit with her friends, she discovers an email message from you that offers her a free guide to giving real estate. She clicks on the link driving her to a landing page where she fills out a form to download the guide and have it emailed to her inbox. Just above the Submit button, she answers a question that seeks to understand how interested she is in such a gift. She no longer states verbatim that she "might consider" such a gift. Instead, she clicks the button signaling that she "is considering" that kind of gift right now.

As she reads the report you thoughtfully offered her, she learns she can also commemorate her husband through a legacy commitment. The report provides commemoration options that include having her husband's name on the donor wall in the lobby of the hospital or on a bench outside the hospital in the garden. For those who give real estate, there are opportunities to name a room or even a wing of the hospital in honor of her husband (depending on the size of the gift). Her *desire* grows even further. In fact, you might say it begins burning as she initiates her search for ways to take *action*.

In this example, the donor has moved herself through the consideration process as a result of the engagement offers she received that were in step with the stage in which she resided, her interests, and the communication channels she preferred. Some of the offers came from the organization and others from you. Either way, the process was seamless and donor-centric. She didn't feel like she was being moved. Instead, she moved herself naturally.

Sharon took action and made the gift. Everyone was happy. As a bonus for the hospital, the commitment was irrevocable. Sharon could not change her gift. She had no intention of doing so anyway. Every time she thought about her decision, she felt good knowing she made the world a better place. For this particular gift, the donor journey concluded.

# It's All About the Relationship

Relationships are the backbone of the consideration continuum. Good relationships support the process as donors move themselves from interest to desire smoothly and effectively, but bad ones can send them running for the hills (or another charity).

One-to-some and one-to-many marketing and fundraising relationships are the same as personal relationships. First and foremost, trust is essential. For example, if you get spammy emails from a company or nonprofit that are impersonal, irrelevant, interruptive, and annoying, you won't trust them because they abused the permission you granted them when you opted in to receive their communications (assuming you opted in at all). If you don't trust them, you won't want a relationship with them anymore, and you certainly won't buy from them or donate to their cause.

There are nine similarities between *marketing* relationships and *real* relationships that must be acknowledged and understood. For both *marketing* relationships and *real* relationships:

- Trust is paramount.

- Offers and communications must be relevant, personalized, and contextual.

- Conversations and dialogue must be informal and relaxed.

- Communications must be two-way, involving talking and listening.

- Exchanges must be respectful, polite, considerate, and fair.

- Both participants must gain value.

- Engagements must be convenient and relaxed.

- Multiple channels of communication (such as phone, email, face-to-face, etc.) must be used.

- Both relationships must be somewhat strategic (in other words, they must have a good reason to exist).

If you keep these concepts in mind, the relationship your donors want is not difficult to attain. For example, imagine you want to go to the movies with someone. It's doubtful you'd ask someone you don't trust, and you probably wouldn't ask them to a movie you know they won't like. When you make the invitation, you wouldn't use formal language, saying, "Would you care to accompany me to a cinematic feature?" Of course not! You'd use colloquial language instead of sounding like a lawyer.

After you invite your friend, you'd give them an opportunity to respond. You'd be fair, polite, and respectful. You'd want to gain something from the experience even if it's simply to have fun or pass the time with someone whose company you enjoy. You'd accommodate one another to make it easy and convenient. You might use multiple channels beginning with some emails to make arrangements and ending with a phone call as you try to find each other in the parking lot. Finally, the whole experience would have some kind of strategic purpose. Let's face it, people don't make friends unless they believe the relationship satisfies their needs in one way or another, in the short term or the long term.

Of course, all of this is common sense. Most marketing is common sense. Unfortunately, common sense is not all that common. Something funky happens when people get the chance to send out mailers or emails to thousands of constituents. It's sort of like what happens when some people get in their cars and lose their humanity. I'm always amazed at how otherwise reasonable, caring, loving people become maniacs behind their windshields, cursing and making obscene gestures.

Similarly, when people get a chance to blast out emails or send letters, they suddenly lose their ability to feel empathy for the recipients of their messages. They become narcissists. They think their target audience will accept the kinds of messages they wouldn't want to receive. They get spam-happy. Too often the result is transactional messages or other types of off-putting communications that seek to force the process to move faster.

If only people remembered that marketing relationships are like real relationships, the reception to their outreach efforts would improve dramatically. They may instinctively know that all relationships follow a similar pattern, but they bury reason, discount logic, or eschew good sense because all they have to do is press a button or sign another purchase order.

Every relationship has a beginning and middle. Many have an ending. In fund-raising, we often call the coming-together part *acquisition* and *early cultivation*. For major and legacy gifts, I prefer *lead generation* (to inspire supporters to lean in to attain value) and *qualification* (to make sure they want to have a deeper, more personal relationship with a fundraiser or their charity's mission). Hope-fully, they'll hire you to help them achieve their goals and the relationship will plateau at the maintenance level. Fundraisers might call this *retention* or *stew-ardship*. Finally, if the relationship deteriorates, it will break apart. Fundraisers call this *lapsing* or *LYBUNTS* (last year but not this year), but the truth is they *fired* you and *defected*.

**How donor relationships with fundraisers
come together and fall apart.**

Remember, according to the Fundraising Effectiveness Project, the average nonprofit's first-time donor retention rate is only 32 percent (just 17 percent for new donors giving under $100). They also determined the five-year aver-age for donor forfeiture in the nonprofit sector to be as follows: for every 100 donors gained, 102.6 were lost, and for every $100 gained, $94.80 was lost.

To say the bucket is leaky is an understatement. But you can plug the holes! Once acquired, most supporters truly don't ever want the relationship to end. They became involved for a reason. They may be testing things out but they're hopeful you'll treat them well. They want you to ask questions about them to understand their needs and wants. Then they want your mission to fulfill them.

Unfortunately, most nonprofits drop the ball. Newly acquired, low-dollar donors stop giving immediately because the après-giving experience is less than rewarding. Instead of a warm and thoughtful follow-up, charities are often cold. For example, after giving to a newly discovered charity online, I received an emotionless tax receipt.

I worked very hard to earn the money I gave to this charity. I felt good as I clicked the buttons online because starting any new relationship is exciting. The next minute was somewhat deflating.

My Gmail notification popped up telling me I had a new message. I opened the email to find a message that mainly encouraged me to do more for them by creating a personal fundraising page online. Really? No offer to take a donor survey? No links to amazing research findings, cures, or success stories made possible by donors like me? No testimonials from beneficiaries of these kinds of donations? No opportunities to sign up for e-newsletters about new treatments? I didn't get a chance to opt in for any of those kinds of communications. Oddly enough, I got them anyway—without giving them my permission. Would you give again after such an experience?

On the other end of the spectrum from new low-dollar donors is legacy givers. Most organizations jump for joy after hearing that a supporter included their organization in their estate plan. But what comes next? Do they call to say thank you? Do they work hard to learn why the donor included the organization in their plan? Do they try to determine what else the charity could do to help them find meaning in their life? Do they aim to provide even more value to them? In my experience, too often the answer to all of these questions is "no." This lack of engagement only serves to increase the likelihood that those same supporters will fire you and the organization and defect. They'll remove the charity from their plans, especially during the last few years of life when so many of us make our final arrangements. Ignoring your donors after they give or make a commitment to give is like ignoring your teeth: doing so makes them go away.

Even small investments in fine-tuning your stewardship efforts can reap massive rewards. Trust, relevance, two-way dialogue, respect, fairness, value, and convenience make donors feel good and help build relationships. Engagement fundraisers recognize that the key to long-term funding success is tied directly to ensuring that *marketing* relationships are the same as *real* relationships.

# It's About Their Relationship with the Mission, Not with You

Now that we know how important it is to build relationships, I have to take issue with fundraisers who puff out their chests saying that fundraising, especially legacy gift fundraising, "is all about the relationship." I don't buy it. I've asked those same people the following: "How many legacy gifts did your organization receive last year that 'came over the transom' and were not previously disclosed to you before you got the money or the call from the attorney?"

The answer is always something like, "70 percent, 80 percent, or 90 percent."

So, if it's "all about the relationship," why didn't they know about so many of those legacy gifts? You simply can't say that legacy gift fundraising is "all about the relationship" if you have no idea about the vast proportion of gifts that have already been planned for your nonprofit. It doesn't add up.

Fundraisers need to stop kidding themselves and giving themselves too much credit. Your personal relationship with a supporter, advocate, or member will certainly affect their legacy giving decisions. Solid, personal, one-to-one relationships are essential. However, the truth is that the donor wants to build a relationship first and foremost with *the organization and its mission* (at least 70, 80, or 90 percent of the time), not necessarily with the fundraiser.

Along the same lines, fundraisers need to realize that donors prefer to have polyamorous relationships with their charities. In other words, your supporters will cheat on you. They will cozy up to other organizations (your competitors). They'll come and go when they please. Sometimes they'll get more engaged and involved with you, and sometimes they'll withdraw or detach. It's up to them. Your supporters are in charge. They control the relationship and the only way you can influence it is by consistently delivering value that surpasses expectations.

Donors will continue the relationship with your organization only if they trust it, believe in its mission, and feel loved. The question is: What are you doing to build and maintain that relationship, grow their trust, and develop their belief in your mission? How are you using technology to multiply yourself so you can engage more supporters to help the facilitation and development of deeper relationships with your organization and its mission? If you're secure enough to recognize that you're not the primary reason why your supporters give and that they don't necessarily want a relationship solely with you, then you'll seek better ways to engage so you can help them feel good and find meaning in their lives.

# But Do They Want To Have a Relationship with You?

If you're a major or legacy gift fundraiser, you're probably responsible for a group of donors in your caseload or portfolio. The collection might have been prepared after a review of some transactional data including a donor's recency of giving, their frequency of giving, and the total monetary value of their gifts (also known as RFM).

You might have a team behind you that conducts prospect research. Or you might enlist the help of a wealth screening or predictive analytics and modeling firm to help you identify the best donors for your portfolio. That's great! Identification is an important part of the process for assembling a target list. But the next step, the *qualification* stage, is much more critical. Don't skip it!

Just because a donor matches a certain profile doesn't mean they should be in your portfolio. They might not want to have a personal relationship with you (or any other fundraiser). They might just want an arm's-length relationship with your organization instead. So before a donor is placed on your caseload, you need to qualify them.

Don't be like so many overzealous (or over-pressured) fundraisers who skip the qualification stage and jump right into cultivation activities. And don't be like the others who skip both the qualification *and* cultivation stages. I know this happens because at least two or three times a year I receive letters requesting donations of $1,000, $5,000, or more. Letters like those might generate some revenue from a portion of a portfolio, but the other portion might privately balk feeling they shouldn't have been on the list in the first place. Or they might recoil because they were asked for too much without proper cultivation.

**Fundraisers should avoid skipping the qualification and cultivation stages.**

According to Richard Perry and Jeff Schreifels of Veritus Group, for every three donors who might meet your major gift criteria, only one will want to relate with you personally.[6] Having a donor on your caseload costs money. Qualifying them ensures that your efforts will be exponentially more cost-effective. You'll spend a lot less time writing, emailing, and calling people who won't

---

6  Richard Perry and Jeff Schreifels, "Qualifying Donors for Major Gift Caseloads," Veritus Group, last modified June 2016, accessed December 2, 2017, https://veritusgroup.com/qualifying-donors-for-major-gift-caseloads/.

respond and a lot more time communicating with people who've opted in because they not only want to make an impact, but also want to work with you to achieve their goals.

And by the way, just because two out of three might not want to be on your caseload now doesn't mean they'll want to be out forever. It just means not right now. Or it means they don't believe they need to work with a facilitator to meet their needs. In that case, they should still benefit from cultivation and stewardship communications. They should always be updated, thanked, and invited. They should not be smothered, and they certainly shouldn't be harassed. With the right kind of communications, they might someday decide they want to talk to you so they can realize their dreams of making an impact and finding meaning in their life.

So, if you aim to have 100 highly qualified donors on your caseload, you'll need to first identify 300 donors with capacity and passion for your cause. Then you'll need to find a way to determine who among them wants to work with you.

The best way to do that is by conducting one-to-one donor discovery visits. But doing 300 of those would be VERY expensive and VERY time-consuming.

The next best way is to use a donor survey to help the most passionate supporters lean in and help you get to know them. Plus, the very fact that someone took the survey is a qualifier on its own. The answers to the survey questions will help you determine who wants in and who wants out. It will also help you prioritize your personal outreach.

# Chapter 5
# Building Relationships with Technology

So far I've talked about how the world has changed and why the old models don't work. I've explored the antiquated fundraising pyramid and why fundraisers need to recognize that there are really two pyramids. I've also brought forth some private-sector concepts such as the four stages of the sales process (awareness, interest, desire, and action) along with lead generation and qualification. Then I combined this with the two pyramids to reflect the fact that legacy gifts can come from anyone. Plus, I've contrasted the concept of populist fundraising with the exponentially wiser and more cost-effective Pareto principle.

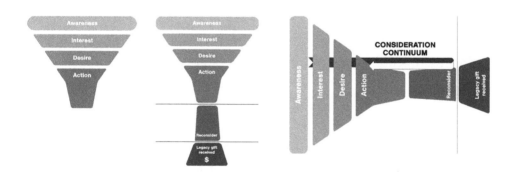

**The original marketing funnel, the marketing funnel for fundraising and a representation of how the consideration continuum entwines with both.**

Additionally, I've spent some time recognizing that most fundraisers are overwhelmed and put in unfair positions with unrealistic demands, while donor expectations have changed and competition for donations has increased. To help them win, I delved into what really makes donors give and explained that fundraisers should employ feedback loops to learn about donor needs, wants, interests, and desires. Then they should use the information they collect to communicate hyper-relevantly to each donor, giving them individual attention and a first-class, VIP experience. I explained six powerful influencers and implored you to become a facilitator, not a fundraiser, by providing value, recognizing the consideration continuum, and focusing on making your organization's supporters feel good while also focusing on donors who opt in to relate to you one-to-one or at arm's length.

All of this sounds good, right? But if I were you, I'd be asking myself, "How on earth am I going to do all of this?" I don't blame you for feeling besieged. If you're like most fundraisers, you're already working hard. You don't have enough time, you're pulled in too many directions, and you're constantly swatting flies. Your board is probably breathing down your neck and your boss is probably on your back!

You care deeply about your organization and its cause, but you're worn out. You know that closing major gifts, uncovering hidden legacy gifts, and migrating mid-level donors to become major donors require your attention. Applying effort there requires massive amounts of donor empathy combined with patience and persistence, but the beneficiaries of your mission, along with your leadership, can't wait. They want results now.

So, how can you win? How can you give everyone what they want? How can you build meaningful relationships with lots of high-value donors and prospects while maintaining your sanity and getting home in time to be with your family and go to bed?

The answer is simple: leverage technology!

We are in the midst of the digital age manifested by the information and communication revolution. Digital devices are everywhere, including desktop computers, tablets, smartphones, smart watches, and so on. Mass media, which traditionally included radio, TV, print publications, and direct mail, now faces competition from direct communication methods including email, text messaging, and social media messaging, webinar tools, video telephony (such as FaceTime or Skype), and so on.

What's amazing about the digital age is the ease with which savvy marketers can leverage technologies to communicate effectively and efficiently with constituents. New technologies are being developed almost daily to help you get the right messages to the right people at the right times. The trick is to understand which technologies to use and how to use them to raise exponentially more money at lowest cost.

# Actionable Intelligence

You probably already have plenty of data in your donor relationship management software (your database) that includes donation recency, frequency, and monetary value. You might also already track involvement information (participation in events, volunteerism, board leadership) and interaction information (notes from discussions collected during donor calls and visits). Although all of that data can help you understand your supporters to a certain extent, none of it is truly actionable. What you really want is *actionable intelligence*—information that can help you focus your activities and costs on the people who will most likely make the greatest financial impact the soonest.

As discussed previously, engagement fundraisers collect actionable information from two data points: verbatims and digital body language. Verbatims are what your supporters say. Digital body language is what they do (online).

Most major gift fundraisers are still using archaic, time-consuming, and expensive strategies to collect verbatims. They call or email supporters to begin the "coming together" stage of the relationship. But getting the attention of your high-value supporters is no easy task. According to Jerold Panas, author of the top-selling fundraising book *Mega Gifts*, "It is a plain fact of fundraising that it's often far more difficult to get an appointment than the gift."[7] Just because they've donated in the past doesn't guarantee they want a deeper relationship with a fundraiser or the mission they represent.

Nonetheless, if the fundraiser gets the chance to meet with a supporter, they'll build rapport and attempt to conduct a "donor discovery" by asking questions designed to help get to know, understand, and qualify the prospect. Conducting one-to-one donor discovery discussions are tremendously effective if you have the time and the staff available to secure and conduct them.

Don't put too much confidence in them, however. Unfortunately, sometimes a discovery visit leads to an "oil and water" situation. The personality of the fundraiser (through no fault of their own) might turn the donor off, sending them to seek out a relationship with a similar yet competitive charity. This is what happened between me and the fundraiser from my alma mater when he asked me to join him for a cup of coffee and an update about the school.

There is another way to conduct donor discovery. Engagement fundraisers save massive amounts of time and money by leveraging technology to collect actionable intelligence using donor discovery surveys. Effective donor surveys capture verbatims by asking supporters about their needs, wants, interests, and desires using convenient channels including digital (email or online), print (usually direct mail), or telephone. Donors prefer to begin the relationship this way thanks to its arm's-length nature. Fundraisers prefer them because they're low-cost, low-effort self-qualifiers that attract the most passionate supporters who respond to them to get involved and provide their personal feedback.

It's a very efficient system, but it's not always perfect. For instance, there's a problem with verbatims: what donors say isn't always true. My firm, MarketSmart, has seen many cases when supporters said they would never make a legacy gift to an organization. Yet, years later, those same supporters actually do make a legacy gift. Apparently, they wanted to keep that information to themselves. That's why it's important to collect the other data point: digital body language.

---

7  Jerold Panas, *Mega Gifts: 2nd Edition, Revised & Updated* (Medfield, MA: Emerson & Church Publishers, 2005), page 71.

Digital body language is the truth serum that helps fundraisers capture the rest of the story (360-degree insights) by monitoring what supporters do online. MarketSmart first pioneered the use of digital tracking cookies for the purpose of monitoring donor behaviors online in 2009.

Digital body language is powerful information. Even better, it's easy to collect at low cost and can help you improve your effectiveness dramatically when it's measured and evaluated. Over time, you can monitor clicks, time on site, and the frequency of each of your supporter's engagements on web pages or social media. Smart fundraisers use this information to spot trends so they can study donor personas and develop highly engaging offers that appeal to small sets of extremely wealthy and highly passionate supporter segments. Even smarter fundraisers use it to generate leads and qualify them.

The monitoring of digital body language can also enable instant value creation for donors in real time. Thanks to the dynamic nature of web pages, your donor's clicks and click histories can be used to instantly and seamlessly serve up highly relevant emotional or informative online content that reflects each individual's unique interests. Isn't that the kind of VIP experience major donors deserve?

For the fundraiser, the recency of each individual donor's engagements provides signals as to when they might be most likely to accept outreach. Our clients, for instance, monitor their dashboards to see which supporters are "hot." The dashboard is a customized online tool that consolidates and arranges results so the client can monitor verbatims and digital body language. Then they call, email, or even message potential donors on Twitter, Facebook, or LinkedIn using highly personalized, relevant, and contextual communications that make their supporters feel good because they were heard and respected.

Fundraisers tell us the difference before and after using these queues for out-reach is like night and day because now they don't have to interrupt donors to talk to them about giving. Now, when they reach out, the donors feel that the timing is terrific. It feels more natural and helpful instead of bothersome and disruptive. It feels like outstanding customer service.

Reaching out at the right time, when donors are ready for their desire to be converted to action, makes all the difference. The seamlessness of the process results in larger donations. and the organization saves time and money.

Verbatims and digital body language provide for low-cost and highly effective digital feedback loops. They speed up the donor discovery process and make it more measurable so it can be analyzed and improved. The future of cost-efficient, donor-centric fundraising depends on this kind of actionable intelligence.

The best fundraisers aren't asking themselves whether or not they'll employ it. Rather, they're asking themselves *when*.

# Progressive Profiling

Fundraisers, as well as their organization's leadership and board members, need to come to terms with the fact that donors make decisions based on *their* timing, needs, wants, desires, and interests, not your organization's. The next step is retooling all marketing efforts to provide engagement offers that will appeal to each supporter in a way that's meaningful to them based on where they are in the consideration continuum.

Fundraisers who acquiesce to this paradigm stop trying to move donors through the consideration process. Instead, they provide highly relevant, valuable offers that are precisely aligned with each donor's "Rubik's Cube" in relation to where they reside in the vortex of the donor journey.

As donors accept and engage with these offers, it's important to capture more and more actionable intelligence—verbatims and digital body language. Doing so helps you understand who they are now, what they want now, how likely they are to give now (or soon), and what you should do now.

The actionable intelligence you collect also helps you monitor them and capture new information about them as they make their way through the donor

journey. This is called *progressive profiling*. Amazon.com does th
anyone. As you search for items online, they monitor your searches
comments to instantly and seamlessly recommend items that are hi
to interest you. We've all come to expect the Amazon level of service
shop online.

Similarly, your donors have come to expect that level of personalization and relevance. They don't necessarily expect it to be as instantaneous, but they do expect you to listen to them and "show 'em that you know 'em." This is a basic truth in the digital age. Ignore it at your own peril.

Engagement fundraisers continuously employ progressive profiling techniques and technologies to understand their donors better and give them the experiences they deserve. At a minimum, I recommend you survey your high-value donors every year. By doing so, you'll see who's moving closer to needing one-to-one contact and who isn't, who once said they might consider a legacy gift and now wants to meet with someone, and who once said they might consider naming opportunities but are now ready to take action.

Once again, you can leverage technology to progressively profile your supporters. Surveys work great, but it's also important to use forms on landing pages to collect verbatims while using tracking tools to collect digital body language over time.

When you boil down Engagement Fundraising to its core, it's about making offers of valuable content patiently and persistently to engage people until they're ready to meet with a facilitator to build a relationship or make a gift. The content can take the form of a video, a quiz, a game, an e-book—the list is endless, as long as it's personal and valuable to that individual. It should be nonthreatening. It should be educational and informative. It should be emotional and entertaining. It should be available and convenient. It *should not* ask for money. It should simply satisfy their needs and, above all else, make them feel good!

As you understand each supporter's individual profile, you should use technology to deliver ongoing, highly relevant, personalized outreach. Every offer for engagement should provide value in relation to what the prospect told you (and did) in the past and is telling you (and doing) now. Alongside every donor-centric communication, you should also provide opportunities for the donor to move herself to the next step of the consideration process, eventually moving herself to take action by giving.

For example, one campaign we recommend in certain cases offers supporters who previously took a donor survey an opportunity to see the aggregate results in a downloadable PDF report filled with charts and graphs. For those who previously said they might give, we include in the form on the landing page a question asking where they are in the consideration process now. Have they made their decision? Do they need help? Are they interested in talking to a facilitator? Or, have they decided against giving altogether? Using technology to gather that information from hundreds or thousands of progressively profiled, high-capacity constituents who previously opted in for communications helps fundraisers prioritize their outreach.

Without technology, it would be almost impossible for a human to implement a successful progressive campaign in a cost-effective way. But now, artificial intelligence can help to understand where the prospect is in the consideration process. Then automation can "drip" the right engagement offers over a long period of time to support the donor's journey as they move themselves from awareness to interest to desire and, finally, to action.

If you were a fundraiser at my university seeking donations for a new building, a progressive campaign might look like this: The first step might be an offer (seemingly from you) to see if I'd like a digital version of my yearbook from my graduation year. Maybe I hadn't thought of the university in a while. Perhaps I lost my yearbook. But wouldn't it be great to get a digital version so I could share pictures with old friends on Facebook?

That offer would get me into the *awareness* stage of the donor journey. It would seriously tweak my memories and pull on my heartstrings. Finally, it would set in motion the unbelievably persuasive law of reciprocity. Of course, when I fill out the form on the landing page, your technology would drop a tracking cookie on my browser (just like Amazon and almost every other private-sector marketer). The form could also ask about my interests to see if I might consider taking a tour of campus someday in the future. I say, "Yes, I might do that."

Later, my *awareness* could be moved to *interest* when I receive another personalized email (seemingly from you) inviting me to sign up for a tour of a building that housed my journalism classes when I was there. The fundraiser (or her database) knew I majored in journalism, right?

Feeling good thanks to your courteous outreach, I sign up and take the tour. As we walk together, we build rapport and chat. You're happy and so am I. There's no pressure or friction. After all, I came to you. I wanted to! I opted in and you were there to facilitate an experience that was designed to make me feel good.

During my tour, I notice the journalism building is 30 years older than when I was taking classes there. Go figure! It's now in disrepair and the air conditioners don't work. Nevertheless, I put the thought aside as so many of my college memories come back. I recount how I met my best friends there and where I hung out with the girl who would become my wife.

Later, while I'm helping my daughter with her homework, I think to myself, "It's really a shame that the old building is in such bad shape." I still brush aside the thoughts because I'm busy.

A few weeks later, I get another personal email (seemingly from you) followed by a touching letter in the mail mentioning that the school is considering a renovation to restore the journalism building back to its old glory. Both the email and the letter give me an opportunity to see an image of what the architect believes the "before and after" result will be. I click on the photo to be led to videos of current students talking about their aspirations. Instantly I feel warmth as my *interest* is moved to a *desire* to help. Beside the images and videos online, I notice there are naming rights available for the new building, its rooms, the lobby, and even for the benches outside. I click to learn more.

While I'm doing this, your technology is following my progress online. I'm ready. So you call me—and I'm really glad you did. We talk a bit, you explain some details, and I pledge my support. My *desire* has been moved to *action,* thanks to you.

Best of all, I feel good. I was empowered to make an impact and the experience was absolutely seamless. Almost all of the communication was done at low cost digitally, the channel I prefer. The offers provided opportunities for me to lean in and engage further. It was all about me. You satisfied my needs first, not the university's. Your communications and offers enabled me to self-inform and self-solicit while you facilitated the process at just the right time.

That's Engagement Fundraising using progressive profiling. It works because it allows people the opportunity to self-direct their own mini-actions over time and turn them into big actions (maybe big donations) later with your help.

# You Can Say That Again!

People are busy. They're also drowning in information, data, marketing, and fundraising communications. Gaining their attention isn't easy. Is it even possible to break through the noise? If you become patient and repetitive you will benefit from signaling theory, the mere exposure theory, and the Baader-Meinhof Phenomenon.

*Signaling theory,* first mentioned by Anthony McGann and Raymond Marquardt at the University of Wyoming in 1975, states that communication messages with high rates of repetition signal quality to consumers, which leads to high ratings in *Consumer Reports*. Donors invest in quality nonprofits in which they believe and have confidence. Therefore, it is highly likely that repetition of the right kinds of messages over time will signal to donors that your organization is a worthy beneficiary of their donations.

Similarly, *the mere exposure theory* states the opposite of the old saying, "familiarity breeds contempt." In marketing and communications, familiarity as a result of repetition often leads to a positive impression and a preference for a brand, or nonprofit—not contempt.

Finally, the *Baader-Meinhof Phenomenon* relates to how, after we first take notice of something, it begins to pop up everywhere. For instance, soon after my next-door neighbor bought a Jeep Wrangler, I began to see Wranglers everywhere I went.

These concepts only reinforce what Thomas Smith wrote way back in 1885 in his groundbreaking book, *Successful Advertising*. It went something like this:

| Number of times seeing an ad | Prospect's reaction |
|---|---|
| 1st time | Doesn't see it |
| 2nd time | Notices it |
| 3rd time | Conscious of its existence |
| 4th time | Faintly remembers having seen it before |
| 5th time | Reads it |
| 6th time | Turns up nose at it |
| 7th time | Reads it and says, "Oh brother!" |
| 8th time | Reads it and says, "Here it is again!" |
| 9th time | Wonders if it matters |
| 10th time | Asks others about it |
| 11th time | Wonders why it matters |
| 12th time | Figures it must be a good thing |
| 13th time | Begins to believe it might be worth considering |
| 14th time | Remembers wanting to take action |
| 15th time | Yearns to take action |
| 16th time | Decides to take action someday |

| 17th time | Makes a conscious decision to take action |
| 18th time | Gains a burning desire to take action |
| 19th time | Considers the decision very carefully |
| 20th time | Takes action |

For charities, it isn't a matter of repeating the same message over and over again. It's about making your donors *feel good* over and over. That's what does the trick.

Repetition costs money, so it's important to try to do it at low cost—while remembering that no one likes the friend who only calls when he needs money! Make sure your repetitive messages are focused on making the donor feel good, and you're not always showing up with your hand out.

Polite, respectful, helpful persistence pays off. Find a balance between being the obliging friend who reaches out every once in a while to provide assistance and the annoying salesperson who won't stop knocking on their door. Making your messages relevant, personalized, novel, and valuable usually takes care of this.

At MarketSmart, we find that many people sign up for my blog posts (sent every Monday, Wednesday, and Friday), our MajorGiftMotivator (free motivational quotes sent out every Tuesday), and our invitations to take advantage of our webinars and free resources. In some cases, our subscribers might get as many as seven email messages from us in a single week, yet few people unsubscribe. That's because our messages provide value. If you do the same, you can send as many messages as you want yet still be reasonably assured that people will not get annoyed.

# Chapter 6
# Don't Ask — Offer!

Most nonprofits focus too heavily on *asking* and don't *give* enough to their supporters. Low donor retention rates reflect this imbalance.

If offers are catalysts that stimulate engagement, interest, and consideration, why isn't more emphasis placed on them? Perhaps it's because the nonprofit's staff has a hard time recognizing why offers are needed and how they work to raise money. I've heard fundraisers admit that their concept of offers was based on retail offers like two for one, 40 percent off, and buy one get one free. How in the world could that apply to fundraising?

Some fundraisers wonder why we need offers at all. I once heard a marketing coordinator at a nonprofit say, "I thought we're supposed to be asking and they're supposed to be giving." The irony is that nonprofits that give to their supporters inspire reciprocation in donations that far exceed the cost of the original gift. If you give, you get!

## Creating Powerful Offers

Fundraising offers are powerful because an exchange of money only happens if some value is provided in return. Pure altruism doesn't exist in philanthropy. Even anonymous donors get value in the satisfaction of knowing their anonymous gifts are helping others.

Some fundraisers involved in direct marketing know the value of providing offers— but instead of delivering value aimed at major donors, they provide it to new and low-dollar donors. The most familiar example comes in the form of personalized address labels that cost pennies to produce but might yield an average donation of around $100, a big return on investment.

Remember, the reciprocation (the donation) generally far exceeds the cost of the original gift. Fundraisers who provide high-value offers for their high-value donors generate exponentially greater dollars at very low costs.

Sadly, many midlevel donors, legacy society members, and even major donors go long stretches without receiving offers. Even a thank you note can be considered an offer. A simple note provides donors the opportunity to reminisce about their own greatness for having done something good to improve the world.

Decades ago, Jerold Panas touched on the importance of gratitude and how it makes donors feel good in his classic 1984 fundraising book, *Mega Gifts*. Panas wrote about an experience he had with a zoo's board member named Mary G. Roebling. Mary once admonished the fundraising team (including Jerry), saying, "Now, Jerry, one thing you must remember. People like to be thanked, they want to know that what they have done is appreciated, really appreciated. When we get a gift that we think is special, let's find a way to thank the person at least seven times before we ever ask them again for another gift."[8]

Because she was a major donor, Mary knew what it felt like to be thanked, appreciated, and offered opportunities for more engagement. She also knew that the more she received from fundraisers, the more she became inspired to give again. She understood that donors like her want something in exchange for their cash even though they often won't admit it.

Still wondering how to know what your donor wants? Step into their shoes. Your offer should facilitate the decision-making process by showing prospective donors how they will benefit and what's in it for them. Help prospects think about how to have a meaningful life, how to deal with their digital inheritance, how to pass on their legacy (ethics, morals, lessons learned), how to tell their story. Tap into the emotions of your supporters.

---

8  Ibid., page 57.

# Three Things to Do Before the Ask

Jerold Panas's story about the importance of gratitude compelled me to come up with a simple methodology to help fundraisers maintain a "giving" mindset. The "3-to-1 Major Gift Fundraising" tool helps fundraisers focus on offers. For every single donation you receive from a major supporter you should 1) thank them, 2) report on the results, and 3) provide an engagement offer before asking for another gift.

To put this idea into action, you simply write down the donor's name. Then, after you send your personalized, heartfelt letter of gratitude, you can put a "check" in the box beside the words "thank you."

Next, find a way to report to your donor what happened with their gift. What was the impact? Be honest. Be transparent. Be real. Personalize it as much as possible. Once you've done that, put a "check" in the box next to the words "report on results."

**1 Thank You + 1 Report on Results + 1 Engagement Offer = Ask for Next Gift**

Last, reach out to offer your donor a meaningful engagement experience. Perhaps you could email her a chance to view a video of your program staff doing great things as a result of her support, or you might send her a note written by someone she helped. Once you have provided that engagement offer, you can put a "check" in the box next to the words "engagement offer." After all three check boxes have been marked, you can consider asking for another gift. I bet you'll get it.

Would you like some of these pads? My staff ships them to fundraisers all over the world for free. Simply order them online at www.imarketsmart.com/321.

Trust me on this. Focus less on their money. You'll reach your goals faster and at lower cost if you focus more on giving them offers to help them satisfy their needs and desires.

# Make Your Offers Opaque

People generally avoid thinking about giving away their money while they're alive. To most, decreasing what's been earned and saved as a result of decades of perseverance and hard work is unnatural. Giving money away isn't easy.

Andrew Carnegie once said, "I resolved to stop accumulating and begin the infinitely more serious and difficult task of wise distribution." Carnegie was born in 1835. But it wasn't until 1889 that he began to devote himself to efforts to give his money away. He was 54. It was then that he wrote the now famous article in the June issue of the *North American Review* titled the "Gospel of Wealth" in which he proclaimed that the rich should use their wealth to benefit society. Carnegie said before his retirement, "I couldn't imagine what I could ever do with so much money."

Unfortunately, many people today aren't of the same mindset. Many wealthy people have financial advisors who mostly recommend monetary growth and preservation tactics. They see their role as one that helps their clients keep and grow their money, not give it away.

There's another reason people try to avoid discussing legacy giving: thoughts and conversations about making bequests conjure up images of their own death.

The best way to overcome these obstacles is to make your offers opaque so supporters only see and consider what's right in front of them.

Without opaque offers, fundraising can be like diving into shallow water. It might seem like a good idea until you bang your head on the bottom. By then it's too late. Your offers will have sounded like asks. People will feel pressured, shamed, and embarrassed.

Don't be fooled by thought leaders who profess that the number-one reason why people don't give is because they weren't asked. It's not about asking, it's about facilitating, and facilitating only involves asking when the time is right. Pressing your supporters to give early in the process will backfire without first delivering opaque offers for engagement.

Wondering what an opaque offer looks like? Software companies like mine are famous for providing opaque offers mostly at the awareness and interest stages of the customer journey. They include free reports, webinars, apps, widgets, and more to get potential customers into the funnel and move themselves forward in the decision-making process. We recognize that we can't ask a potential buyer to make a major decision right away. So we take it slow. We deliver opaque offers that satisfy needs further away from the final outcome we hope to achieve.

One such offer is the MajorGiftMotivator series we mentioned earlier. We know that fundraisers combat rejection daily. They need motivation to keep going. So we created an automated system that sends fundraisers (who opt in, of course) a single, powerful motivational quote once a week, every Tuesday morning. The quotes are from leaders in the field, tailored for major gift fundraisers. You can sign up for them at www.imarketsmart.com/majorgiftmotivator.

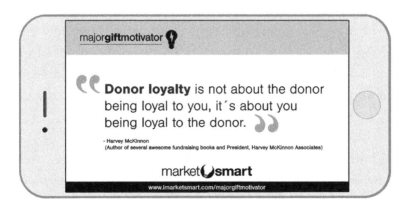

**An example of one of our weekly major gift motivational quotes.**

This offer helps fundraisers help themselves. It provides value and it makes them feel good. It also aligns perfectly with the target audience we hope to attract and builds goodwill among a solid list of high-value potential customers. Later, when the time is right, we might ask them to buy from us, but not at the beginning of the process. First, we provide opaque offers so they'll stay focused solely on satisfying their own needs.

It works in major and legacy gift fundraising, too. Just like our potential customers, potential donors need to first clearly see the value, reward, or benefit of leaning in. The early offers must be opaque and solely align with value they'd appreciate based on where they are in the consideration process.

Talking to donors too soon about making a major gift or bequest will typically cause them to avoid the subjects. Remember, reducing one's net worth is usually perceived as a losing proposition, and planning a bequest often reminds people of their impending doom. These are not impulse decisions. Like marketing high-value software or services, you have to employ a long-term engagement strategy that recognizes where people are along the consideration continuum and provides value to make people feel good every step of the way.

Opaque offers wrap donor engagements in positivity to help them take small steps forward. They cloak the issue of giving for everyone's benefit. For instance, we've found that major and legacy prospects appreciate opaque offers that help them involve themselves with information about how they can become philanthropic, make an impact, or live on in the minds of others after their lifetimes. These offers are not about giving or making a bequest. They don't remind people about reducing their net worth or their own demise. Instead, they're the sugar that helps the medicine go down.

You and I both know that giving, like medicine, can make people feel good. Without sweet, opaque offers preceding an ask, however, solicitations seem blatant and unpleasant to a donor—like medicine that leaves a bitter aftertaste.

At MarketSmart, we offer around two dozen varied and "productized" offer campaigns that work well with our platform and can be tailored for individual organizations and "sweetened" with more or less opacity as needed. More opacity is needed at the early stages of the consideration process. Alternatively, when donor desire is burning and they're ready to take action, the offers can be much less opaque. At that point the asks can be more blatant and straightforward.

One successful productized offer we provide our clients that works well at every stage of the consideration process is a legacy journal workbook, *The Memoir Maker*. You can develop an offer like this yourself to provide value for your donors. Here's how it works:

- You reach out to your supporters offering to help them think about their autobiography, and what they want to pass on to their family and friends.

- The help comes in the form of a personalized and branded workbook they can use to ask themselves questions about their life story and how they want to be remembered.

- The workbook also encourages your supporters to think about and list which causes are important to them and why.

- There is no ask.

- The workbook can be mailed to them or downloaded as a PDF online.

This offer works for a wide range of supporters including midlevel, major, or legacy cohorts. It develops awareness and interest in your organization while building trust and a desire to reciprocate. It also helps to facilitate engagement while encouraging donors to tell you about themselves, their needs, and their desires.

Another offer is the *Tell Your Story Campaign*. It's an opportunity for donors to tell how their life narrative and mission entwines with the mission of the organization. For example, a donor to the Ocean Conservancy might write about his fun memories of going to the beach and fishing with his grandfather since he taught him to care about the creatures of the ocean, and he wants to help preserve those creatures' habitat. That's a story he'd like to share and doing so helps entwine him with your mission even more. Once he's finished typing he can even upload a photo of his grandfather. Of course, we ask permission to post the stories or use them on social media. Then, others read them and the stories trigger similar feelings as they, too, entwine their positive emotions forever with the Ocean Conservancy and its mission. In the end, the donors' relationships with the brand become expanded as their sense of community is invigorated.

Need an offer for donors with a burning desire to take action? One of our clients was involved in a capital campaign with a goal of funding a $26 million construction project. They wanted to rebuild a hall on campus that was first constructed back in 1964 when the college had only biology, chemistry, and physics majors and just 750 students. Now they have more than 1,800 students and 10 science and engineering majors. The new building includes a 60,000-square-foot renovation as well as a 40,000-square-foot addition, making it a perfect opportunity for donors to gain notoriety by naming rooms, halls, and even the entire building.

We suggested they offer donors who are ready an online interactive tool that includes architectural drawings. The tool helps donors visualize their names on parts of the new building. If they want to learn more, they can fill out a form to talk to a Gift Officer about the offer right away.

Valuable offers like these have the potential to reach wider audiences. They can sometimes be more powerful than direct asks, especially if you remember that value is in the eye of the beholder. Step into their shoes and make sure the right offers reach the right donors at the right times.

Stop offering prospects things they don't want. For instance, stop offering them a chance to be in your legacy society unless the membership provides real benefits. Stop offering estate planning financial calculators that hardly anyone understands (except lawyers and CPAs). Also, for goodness' sake, stop offering a cup of coffee so you can update them on what's going on.

Instead, craft offers aligned with your supporters' needs and entwine them with your mission. Help them find meaning in their lives and feel good. Facilitate the decision-making process by showing them how they'll benefit and what's in it for them. Support their desire to tap into their own emotions. Connect their life narrative to the problem and the solution. Give to them first with a focus on where they are in the consideration process, their needs and desires—not their money—and your donors will want to become your partner.

Soon enough, their major gifts and legacy gifts will require your assistance and facilitation. The amounts involved and the legal and tax considerations will necessitate your involvement and expertise. Once your offers engage supporters enough and make them ready to act, you'll get to roll up your sleeves and do what you do best: meet one-to-one with them to enhance the relationship, facilitate giving, and make the donor feel good!

# Provide Offers That Deliver Value in Line with Needs

You don't "grow out of" diabetes. My wife continues to face the struggles of the disease every day, and we continue to volunteer and donate. We're on the radar of charities that fight the disease, which means we receive their communications, direct mail, and offers. Sometimes they inspire us, sometimes they don't.

Here's one that failed. We received an ask right before the holidays. It was a letter asking for a donation, and it used the law of reciprocity by giving us free Thanksgiving recipes. The letter came from an organization that we cared about deeply and in which we were already interested. In fact, a few years ago I told their Director of Planned Gifts that I included them in our estate plan by beneficiary designation in my life insurance policy.

The outside of the envelope referred to the recipes included inside. That sparked our curiosity. It wasn't a particularly personalized or emotional offer but it was timely. We were happy to receive the communication, so we opened the letter.

It was a great offer except for one thing. The recipes included ingredients she couldn't eat—sugar! Sadly, the diabetes charity sent my diabetic wife and me recipes to make foods she shouldn't eat. My wife looked at me with tears welling up in her eyes. I looked to see why, then grabbed the envelope and threw it in the trash.

Hard to believe, but it's a true story. Their offer delivered no value because it was entirely misaligned with our needs and downright offensive. Although it might have been a good offer for families that don't include diabetics, for us the offer made no sense. I applaud those fundraisers for their employment of opaqueness. But in this case, they dove into shallow water and hit their heads.

Of course, we still want to support organizations funding research for a cure for diabetes, but not necessarily by giving to that organization. That day they left us feeling alienated and annoyed.

To make sure this doesn't happen to you, consider that offers are "boxes" of value that you give to your prospects. What's inside the box should be different yet meaningful in the right way for every donor. No one wants to receive an empty box—or even worse, a box filled with items that are inappropriate and make the person on the other end feel worse than they did before.

Think about your offers before you send them. Don't piss people off. There are real people receiving your letters, emails, and phone calls who are eager to support your efforts. You owe it to them to be considerate and thoughtful. Give them value in line with their needs.

# Focus on Your List

Imagine you live in Miami, Florida, and in November you receive a beautiful, very clever postcard from your local hardware store advertising 50 percent off snow shovels. You visit the store soon after and learn that the marketing department for the chain of stores (located in Chicago) mixed up the lists, sending the wrong offers to the wrong people. The offer was supposed to be sent to people living in Massachusetts where it's cold and snowy. The creative was great, but the list was wrong.

Too often marketers and fundraisers spend way too much time on the creative aspects of direct marketing. Yet the creative is the least important aspect of any approach. I recommend you only spend about 5 percent of your time and money on that component of your direct marketing plan. In fact, an ugly design with the right offer sent to the right audience will beat a beautiful, witty, creative package sent to the wrong list every time. If your list is bad and your offer doesn't resonate and provide value, it won't matter how creative and pretty you designed your outreach and how good the timing is.

First and foremost, what makes offers work best is a *qualified list*. It's the most essential component for the success of any direct marketing plan. You should spend about 60 percent of your effort making sure you have a great list. At MarketSmart, we recommend you collect verbatims and digital body language over time so you can segment your audience properly according to their capacity, their needs, where they reside along the consideration continuum, and so on. Doing so makes the list hyper-qualified.

After the list is pulled and segmented, a *quality offer* is next in importance. Spend at least 20 percent of your time and energy developing offers that draw people in to engage, are highly relevant (thanks to your segmentation), and provide tremendous value in the form of good feelings and relevant benefits.

| 60% | 20% | 15% | 5% |
|-----|-----|-----|-----|
| LIST | OFFER | TIMING | CREATIVE |

**Where you should focus your efforts when creating
direct marketing communications.**

# Match Offers to Donors

Richard Perry, founding partner of Veritus Group, said on his blog:

> In major gifts, the successful MGO (Major Gift Officer) needs to iden-
> tify the interests and passions of the donor, then present a program to
> that donor that matches those interests and passions. Done correctly,
> these activities eventually cause an economic transaction.[9]

I couldn't agree more. You have to find out why they care, what programs they
care about, who they might like to commemorate, and so on. If you match the
donor's needs and interests with an offer that delivers value, you'll engage her
in a way that will be more likely to lead to a gift.

The one thing I would add is that MGOs should leverage technology to identify those interests and passions faster and more cost-effectively. They can also
consider leveraging technology to match the donor's interests and passions
with their programs.

For example, imagine you work for a museum. A previous donor who responded to a survey recently recounted the fact that her mother took her to the
museum as a child and they shared many wonderful afternoons looking at the
exhibits. Her mother passed away last spring. The donor also mentioned that

---

9  Richard Perry and Jeff Schreifels, "Tips on Selling Anything in Major Gift Fundraising," Veritus Group, last modified
   February 17, 2014, accessed December 2, 2017, https://veritusgroup.com/tips-on-selling-anything-in-major-gift-
   fundraising/.

her mother appreciated the fact that the museum held a program for mothers and daughters every Mother's day. In the survey, the donor also said she had jewelry she'd consider giving away. Yes, we've asked this in surveys, and yes, people respond!

Wouldn't it make sense to offer her an opportunity to honor her mother through a commemorative gift that uses the jewelry (which might have been her mother's jewelry) or some other asset to fund an endowment that would keep the Mother's Day program running for all time? That donor doesn't want return address labels. She wants to find meaning in her life. She wants to honor her mother's life, and she wants to make other people's lives better.

Develop these kinds of offers, match them to the right people, and donors will engage.

## Align Offers with the Consideration Continuum

Now, before I go on, remember the 80/20 rule (the Pareto principle). If we're smart as we develop our offers, we're focusing on generating major gifts, encouraging legacy gifts, and moving mid-level donors up. We're also recognizing that donors build relationships with nonprofits the same way they build them with people: slowly!

It takes a long time. People don't suddenly become best friends overnight. It happens through many lightweight engagement experiences instigated by offers that provide value, such as:

"Would you like some company?"

"I'll walk your dog while you're away."

"Want to go see that movie with me?"

Of course, later, if the relationship grows, the offers might become more permanent:

"Would you be my child's godmother?"

It's the same with the relationships people build with nonprofits. That's why you probably won't want to ask for money during the first encounter with a major donor. Now more than ever, your fundraising strategies need to exhibit patience and your engagement offers must align with every stage of the relationship. They must provide value to your supporters based on where they are in the consideration continuum and sync with the outcome you hope to realize from the engagement.

So before you develop an offer, consider:

- What is the outcome I hope to achieve?

- What do I know about the donor or the segment of donors I'm targeting?

- Where are they in the consideration continuum?

- What are their wants, needs, and desires?

- What can I do for them that will provide value based on what I know and what they want?

- And, finally, how does my offer align with all of the above? Will it help support a donor's decision making or facilitate a gift?

Effective Engagement Fundraising offers often provide intangible benefits. They might:

- Make people feel better about themselves.

- Give people the opportunity to learn something new.

- Enable people to get in touch with their personal life mission.

- Allow people a chance to improve themselves.

- Provide them an opportunity to give back.

- Deliver insight into the effectiveness of your programs.

For instance, an offer to make a donation online (designed for people at the action stage of the consideration process) might help someone feel they're making the world a better place. It might give them a warm fuzzy feeling, or, perhaps, help them fulfill a religious obligation.

Alternatively, an offer to watch and share a video about children in an impoverished foreign country getting tons of bottles of clean drinking water might help them feel good about supporting your programs in particular. Or if that offer was aimed at people in the awareness stage, it might be tweaked to inform them of the need that exists—one that your organization solves.

And finally, an offer to download a report about how one can get a tax break and a steady income stream for life while also helping support a charity will give a supporter a chance to improve their current state. That offer should probably be aimed at people who are already aware of your mission and need to either build interest or desire before taking action.

# Make Your Offers Novel

Humans love novelty. That's why car manufacturers continuously update their models, Apple releases updated product enhancements every few months, and McDonald's brings back the McRib sandwich whenever pork prices drop deep enough to ensure profitability.

Providing novelty in the offers you deliver to your supporters can also be exceptionally effective. Novelty can draw forth their engagement and help people move themselves through the consideration process. People are naturally drawn to opportunities to acquire new information or become involved in fresh, new experiences because it makes them feel good.

Proof of why we are drawn to novelty was provided in 2006 by researchers at University College London. They found that novel information and experiences trigger the release of dopamine—the feel-good chemicals—making us feel like there might be a reward waiting just around the corner. Their research suggests that we apparently anticipate positivity in association with novel offers.

They also found that novelty improves memory. By combining novel, new information with familiar information during learning sessions, their subjects' memories of the familiar were boosted by 19 percent. In other words, providing your supporters with new information or new ways of engaging with familiar concepts may help them retain an understanding of your organization's mission, need, and how they can make an impact.

You might be thinking that all this talk about novelty contradicts the research I mentioned previously on repetition. "Don't we want repetition, not novelty?" you might ask.

The key point is that repetition can breed familiarity and trust in your organization, but you will eventually hit a point of diminishing returns. People will get sick of hearing the same message over and over again. With novelty, we're talking about bringing something new into the mix of your offers for engagement. Offers for engagement require novelty to attract attention and to ensure that people become less worn out by your repetitive messages.

The bottom line is that if you want people to engage with you more and remember what your organization can do on behalf of donors like them who want to make an impact, make sure your offers are novel.

# Ask for Engagement

Depending on your strategic objectives, you'll want to employ offers that range from "soft" to "hard." Hard offers ask supporters to take action or make a commitment right now, while soft offers ask supporters to respond or engage in ways that do not require much significant or careful consideration.

Offer "do's":

- Make sure the offer aligns with your mission.

- Design it to add value to your supporter's life.

- Be clear, simple, and specific.

- Tell them what you want them to do.

- State or imply how they will benefit.

- Use the word "you."

- Make it urgent so the reader takes action now.

- Include a call to action.

- Make it easy and convenient.

- For hard offers especially, portray the problem as big but solvable.

You might not be able to accomplish all of these do's in one effort, but you don't have to. The list includes things you should consider as you develop your offers.

And here are some "do nots" you'll want to avoid:

- Avoid being overly creative or clever—hoping your supporters will figure out what you want them to think or do will be unsuccessful.

- At all costs, do not drive people into a brick wall by leaving out a way for them to take action.

- Don't ever be so dramatic that the solution seems unattainable.

Engagement Fundraising is not transactional. It's not about taking someone from the starting line to the finish line in one episode. It's about giving people a low hurdle to overcome in order to get involved. Good Engagement Fundraising offers work because expectations are lowered, making them fair and safe. There's no pressure on the supporter to give money or take some other action. All that's offered is value. You give and they get. Best of all for them, they don't have to give anything in return.

Your offers don't necessarily have to cost much either. They just need to provide a reason for people to engage with your mission in a way that provides value for them because of the relevance to their needs and desires.

Aim to involve people with your offers. It's not about asking for money; not right now. In many cases, asks should be made by Gift Officers anyway. Believe it or not, if you've delivered outstanding offers that've been properly aligned with the donors' needs as they traveled through the consideration process over time, your donors might self-solicit and give on their own. That's a good thing because the cost of donor visits is only going to increase.

Here are some examples of solid Engagement Fundraising offers we've used on behalf of our clients at MarketSmart. There are many more. But this will help you get the idea so you can come up with offers on your own.

# Is Your Offer Worth Sending?

❑ Is it fun?

❑ Is it novel?

❑ Is it fair?

❑ Is it honest?

❑ Are you being transparent?

❑ Is it shareable?

❑ Will it evoke emotion?

❑ Will it make them feel good (release dopamine and/or oxytocin)?

❑ Will it provide a sense of community (connection with others)?

❑ Will it help educate or inform?

❑ Will it help them feel like the hero in their own life story (provide feelings of autobiographical heroism)?

❑ Will it give them a sense that they can live forever in the minds of others (provide feelings of symbolic immortality)?

❑ Will it enable them to give back or pay it forward to others?

❑ Will it give them notoriety and/or praise?

❑ Will it enable them to right wrongs they want to change in society?

❑ Will it give them a feeling that they're being religious or that they may be able to satisfy their religious dictates?

- Sign up for notifications about new blog posts and you'll learn _____.

- Take the survey so you can tell us what you think.

- Volunteer and you could make great new networking contacts (or meet new people, develop new skills, teach your skills to others, feel needed and valued, give back, improve the lives of others, or simply make a difference).

- Share this and your friends will appreciate that you did!

- Give conveniently using your donor-advised fund.

- Make your donations go further when you give to our Challenge Campaign in which a matching grant from a generous major sponsor doubles your gift.

- Tell your story about how and why you share our mission using our new widget and then you can share it (on Facebook or other social media) with your friends.

- Create your autobiography using our fun workbook so you can pass on your views, ethics, values, and story to future generations.

- Create your ethical will using our fun workbook to share your life lessons with your family and friends.

- Learn how to create a will and prepare your estate plan using our free workbook (or by requesting our kit, joining our webinar, attending our seminar, etc.) so you can provide for your loved ones and the charities you believe in.

- Check out our webinars (videos, infographics, bulletins, and/or any other ways to show "what you did with their money") so you can see the impact your donations make.

- Try out our helpful app (widget, game, calculator, locator map, and/or any other ways to help improve your supporters' lives).

- You're invited to attend our science and research event so you can learn how our researchers are using your donations to search for a cure.

- Get a special VIP tour of the facility so you can see firsthand how your donations have built a foundation for successful impact.

- Subscribe to our e-newsletters (advocacy alerts, financial reports, updates, and other news) so you can stay up-to-date.

Effective engagement offers are powerfully self-actuating. They help supporters intrinsically understand that they can make a difference. They help them feel they have a true philanthropic partnership between themselves and your organization because they feel personally valued, involved, and listened to.

Great offers show donors what your organization can help them accomplish if they empower themselves by investing in your organization so together you can make an impact. They reduce the need for uncomfortable asks because they help donors move themselves through the consideration continuum and even solicit themselves. When offers leverage technology to provide value in highly relevant ways that align with the consideration process, prospects self-qualify, self-educate, self-involve, and, finally, self-solicit.

Don't ask so much for money. Ask for engagement. Don't be a fundraiser, be a facilitator. Give offers and you'll get donations.

# Automated Cultivation:
# More Than "Moves Management"

I've never really felt comfortable with the phrase "moves management." If you're unfamiliar with the term, it refers to a process Gift Officers or other fundraising professionals use for moving donors from cultivation to solicitation.

Moves management requires you to develop a strategy and implement a plan for every single donor or prospect on your list. The plan would consist of everything that you would do for, or with, a donor to get them to move through the consideration process and take action. Then the plan would be executed ensuring that the "moves" are made. Of course, the strategy could be readjusted and refined over time with newly formulated moves.

The good news is that the concept is donor-centric (it's about the donor, not just their money). It places emphasis on taking notes to document the moves, which is a good practice for ensuring that the relationship-building process garners the attention and focus it deserves. Finally, it involves gathering information over time (progressive profiling) about a supporter's biography, interests, passions, and giving histories.

What makes me uncomfortable about the phrase is that it seems to place a lot of weight on the Gift Officer "moving" a specific (usually small) set of donors to give within a certain time frame, rather than enabling supporters to move themselves.

Even the term's originator, Dave Dunlop, shares my concern. In an interview with Jim Lord, author of the classic book on fundraising titled *The Raising of Money*, Dave said the term "can easily be misunderstood, so people start 'making moves' and making a game of moves, rather than really recognizing the process we're a part of is inspiring people to do the things that we believe they would want to do anyway. Really helping them accomplish what is consistent with their values and interests."[10]

---

10 Jim Lord, "So I Asked Dave Dunlop: Is "Moves Management" Misunderstood?" The Center for Leadership Philanthropy, last modified January 21, 2016, accessed December 2, 2017, https://leadershipphilanthropy.com/so-i-asked-dave-dunlop-is-moves-management-misunderstood/.

Cultivation is challenging work. It involves gathering massive amounts of information, keeping track of vast quantities of details, writing personal letters and emails, and so forth. Everyone in the business of raising money knows they need to do it, but hardly anyone can afford the time and effort required to do it exceptionally well.

Now the technology exists for attracting interest in major gifts among a larger audience using engagement offers instead of moves. That's why I think it's time to *do more than moves management*. Nonprofits should leverage technology to automate the tedious, time-consuming, inefficient, and expensive cultivation process for their Gift Officers. They'll spend more time with the most highly qualified prospects who want to have a deeper relationship and are ready to meet with a fundraiser skilled in facilitating the exchange of money for value.

Leveraging technology enables you to widen the funnel to create a feedback loop and engage with more major and legacy gift prospects than you ever could on your own. In Engagement Fundraising, the donor is more in control of the process than the fundraiser. With Engagement Fundraising, the donor gets to decide if, when, and where he'll engage.

Don't get me wrong: the old moves management approach works. It's just a clunkier version of what technology can do now for more people, effortlessly. The best approach is a blending of the two. If you let technology handle the moves and provide the offers that empower a donor to move herself through the process, then you can handle the moves necessary to facilitate the giving action once the donor is ready for a deeper relationship and face-to-face contact.

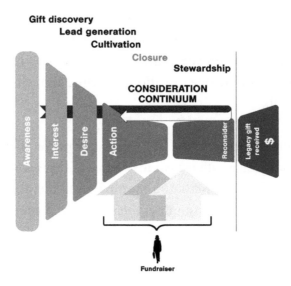

**Gift Officers can be much more efficient and effective if they spend time with supporters who are ready for one-to-one engagement.**

# How MarketSmart Simplifies Cultivation

Engagement Fundraising using the MarketSmart dashboard captures all the data generated from prospects and blends them with an algorithm based on over 20 years of major donor behavior and psychology. This tracking technology assigns an engagement score to show you how engaged prospects are in relation to their likelihood of making a gift. The engagement scoring is based on each supporter's online and offline involvement with an organization's mission. It provides fundraisers with *actionable intelligence* about new donors, repeat donors, and legacy society members.

The system then automates customized, highly relevant drip emails that are personalized by the technology and sent on behalf of the nonprofit in a cadence that's right for each donor. They are usually text-only email "touches" that look like they came directly from a Gift Officer. They provide value. They offer supporters opportunities to engage further by clicking on links that are likely to interest them based on their verbatims, their digital body language, and where they reside along the consideration continuum.

By leveraging technology, engagement fundraisers automate the process of cultivation to save themselves time and money. Donors appreciate the process because it recognizes their desire to engage with your mission at times of their choosing. If they want to learn more at 3:00 A.M. in their pajamas, so be it.

The technology is not a requirement for reaping the benefits of Engagement Fundraising techniques. It just makes it easier, less costly, and more donor-centric. The only real requirement is a mind shift to a new way of thinking about charitable fundraising and technology. It's about leveraging new tools to treat donors fairly. It's about providing valuable offers. It's about engagement. And it's about doing all of that so your organization optimizes its staff to spend most of their time facilitating transactions with people who are ready—not on managing moves.

# The Four Selfs

The beauty of automated cultivation is that the potential donor is in control of choosing when and if to engage with your organization. Remember that donors don't want to be qualified by you. They prefer to qualify themselves. Similarly, they'd like to educate themselves, involve themselves, and solicit themselves. These are the "four selfs" of Engagement Fundraising:

- Self-qualification

- Self-education

- Self-involvement

- Self-solicitation

Just as you and I prefer to opt in to receiving emails from a marketer, donors prefer to opt in to be in your portfolio. Engagement Fundraising recognizes this truth and ensures that portfolios of major and legacy donors include people that have *qualified themselves*.

Of course, the Pareto principle applies here. Those who have been asked to opt in should first have the capacity to give, as well as some passion and interest in your organization's mission. The thing to remember is that Engagement Fundraising should always be permission-oriented. A donor should have the opportunity to decide whether they want to have a deeper relationship with you and your organization, when they'd like it to move forward, and at what pace.

Furthermore, openness and transparency also apply. Imagine the level of trust you'll engender if you turn your organization into a reality show. Imagine if your supporters could see and hear about your struggles as you help your donors maximize their impact. How grateful would they be for your efforts? How trusting would they be once they see how well you accomplish your mission on their behalf or how honest you are about your challenges and failures?

Could reality TV be part of your nonprofit's future? Perhaps that goes too far, but the fact remains that donors today want you to enable their self-education about the impact they can make and how your organization can help them do so. Are you allowing your supporters the chance to *educate themselves* about the things they care about most at times that are convenient for them?

Next is involvement. Are you providing your supporters with opportunities to immerse themselves more deeply in your mission? One of the best ways to generate major gifts is to invite high-capacity supporters to join your board or a committee. Why not ask them to become a non-board-related volunteer?

Volunteerism is the gateway drug leading to major giving and legacy gifts. Proof is offered by statistics from the 2016 U.S. Trust® Study of High Net Worth Philanthropy based on a survey of U.S. households with a net worth of $1 million or more (excluding the value of their primary home) and/or an annual household income of $200,000 or more:

- 42.2 percent of high-net-worth individuals want to learn more about how to identify the right volunteer opportunity for them. Are you helping them pick your organization?

- 49.7 percent of high-net-worth individuals volunteer. Therefore, your best prospects are probably already in your midst, right under your nose.

- 55.9 percent of high-net-worth individuals volunteer at two or more organizations. In other words, they're testing you and comparing you to your competition.

- 84.3 percent give to some, most, or all of the organizations for which they volunteer. They don't just give their time; they give their money, too.

- High-net-worth volunteers give 56 percent more dollars overall than nonvolunteers with similar net worths.[11]

Although volunteerism is a highly effective way to involve high-capacity supporters more deeply in your cause, there are other, more arm's-length offers you can provide. For instance, why not deliver opportunities for them to take a tour, attend a webinar, watch a video, or have any other experience that will make them feel good? The question to ask yourself is, "Are you enabling *self-involvement*?"

Finally, I saved the best for last—*self-solicitation*. Engagement Fundraising helps create circumstances that lead your supporters to ask themselves to act, solve problems, and take stands. Oprah did that when she decided to build a school as she met with Nelson Mandela. John C. Harvard did that in 1638 when he made his deathbed bequest to create the first institution of higher education in the United States.

In the private sector we say, "People don't like to be sold, but they love to buy." Similarly, people don't like to be targets of fundraising, but they love to give. Your efforts need to provide opportunities for self-actualization among your high-capacity supporters so they'll solicit themselves once they have belief and confidence in your mission and your ability to carry it out on their behalf.

---

11 "The 2016 U.S. Trust® Study of High Net Worth Philanthropy: Charitable Practices and Preferences of Wealthy Households," U.S. Trust®, last modified October 2016, accessed December 2, 2017, http://www.ustrust.com/publish/content/application/pdf/GWMOL/USTp_ARMCGDN7_oct_2017.pdf 2016.

# The Digital Donor Concierge

If your organization has 10,000 active donors, it's very likely they'll be categorized as follows:

- A small number will generate 80–90 percent of the revenue.

- Midlevel donors will have a lot of potential for major giving.

- Low-capacity donors will be much less likely to make impact gifts.

- All of the above could make legacy gifts, but 80 percent of the dollars from those gifts will come from 20 percent of the legacy donors.

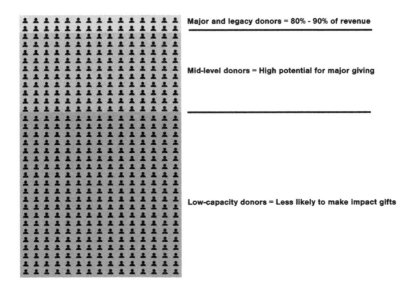

**Breakdown of major, legacy, mid-level and low-capacity donors.**

With that in mind, engagement fundraisers must challenge themselves to optimize how they spend their donors' dollars on performing stewardship functions, cultivation communications, and solicitation efforts. Should they call every single donor after each donation no matter how large or small the gift? Should they send personalized, hand-written thank you letters? Should they visit every single donor and legacy society member? Yes, because donors deserve all of that. But it isn't realistic, right?

It's impossible to provide first-class service and high-quality communications to everyone. So, fundraisers are forced to screen their donor files for capacity, sort them to build portfolios, and write moves management plans. At least that *was* the case.

Enter technology. Donors deserve highly relevant, highly personalized, heart-felt communications, and now they can get it. Technology—more specifically *the digital donor concierge (a virtual steward)*—has now made it possible to provide more supporters with first-class, VIP, "red velvet rope" experiences.

Imagine a very wealthy supporter is in Australia. You're in the United States. A couple of days ago he was on your organization's website reading your blog stories about supporters like him who funded the construction of schools in Africa. Later, at about noon for him (around 8:00 P.M. on Sunday night for you), he gets an email seemingly from you. The email invites him to click on a link to view a live feed streaming video of children playing before their classes begin outside of the school built thanks to his gifts. He clicks on the link, watches the streaming video, and feels terrific. He replies to the automated email he thought you wrote. You're busy helping your kids with their homework and your smartphone buzzes letting you know you just received his message. You briefly skim it and it says:

"Thank you so much for sending me that link. I'd like to fund the construction of another school. Please let me know next steps."

About an hour later as you're putting your kids to bed, you seemingly send him another email without lifting a finger. The message says:

"Terrific. Glad to hear it. Thank you so much. We appreciate you more than you can know. And so do the children. Please click here to see my calendar. Feel free to select a date and time to chat when it's convenient for you."

A bit later as you settle in for a good night's sleep, you get another notification letting you know that he used your appointment-setting widget. He booked the time to talk to you so you can do what you do best: facilitate an exchange of money for value. Congratulations. Another school will be built soon.

Welcome to the future of Engagement Fundraising, the digital donor concierge.

MarketSmart is pioneering technology that makes it possible, through artificial intelligence and machine learning, for fundraisers to become exponentially more efficient and effective. Our clients are benefitting from its efficacy already, but we're just getting started. We aim to help fundraisers zero in on high-capacity supporters already teed up for conversations with you when they have a burning desire to give and are ready to take action.

The digital donor concierge won't replace fundraisers, but it will help them raise more money, faster, and at lower cost. It will help them migrate mid-level donors into major and legacy gift caseloads. It will help them steward major donors and legacy society members. It will do all of this and so much more. It will also give donors the experiences they deserve, and give you more time to live your life.

The digital donor concierge can help support your efforts to deliver offers that are effective and self-actuating. It can help support your efforts to treat supporters well, ensure they receive value or information, and make certain they intrinsically understand that they can make a difference.

Then, when they see the need, they will self-solicit. When they feel personally valued and listened to, they will pay for the privilege to make an impact. Once they understand what your organization can help them accomplish, they will step up, essentially *buying* empowerment to change the world.

# Chapter 7
# Putting It All Together

Is fundraising broken? You decide.

I came to the conclusion that the nonprofit sector needed an overhaul when I was the recipient of fundraising communications as a mistreated donor. I realized people like me want to give but aren't being given what they need—what they deserve.

If you've read this book, chances are you're a fundraiser or are involved in a charitable organization in some way. Chances are you have virtuous intentions and want to do good in the world. Most charities, and the people who work for them, do. Unfortunately, the system is working against you.

For lack of a better solution, you're asked to be marketers or cold-callers, employing skill sets you don't typically have. You're overworked, underpaid, and not succeeding in growing your organization. Even if you're bringing in donations, wouldn't you like to do better?

Too often, you're asked to approach people simply because they're wealthy. It's a tedious and time-consuming process to cultivate a donor and move them through the consideration process. Development can take years, and it becomes even more difficult when there's no continuity in relationships due to the job hopping that seems inevitable.

## Why Engagement Fundraising?

Engagement Fundraising is a better way. It's a solution to a broken system. Until now, most fundraising has been based on "single shot" strategies. For example, it might be an event, gala, or golf outing. Perhaps it's a mailing, an email blast, or a social media campaign. It could even be a face-to-face visit, a tour of your facilities, or a webinar.

You might use multiple channels to promote what you're doing, but the effort will usually target one particular kind of gift and achieve short-term results. A single shot!

Single shots are expensive, time-consuming, and inefficient because they fail to optimize your staff and resources. That's how short-term gains work. As many fundraisers say, "That's the way we've always done it."

But that's not the way it has to be.

Engagement Fundraising is relationship-based, technologically empowered fundraising for the 21st century. Leveraging technology automates lead generation, qualification, and cultivation, and it does so in numbers impossible for an individual to accomplish. The software monitors who is engaging when and what they're doing; then it scores the engagements based on what prospects say (verbatims) and what they do (digital body language). As the donors automatically receive highly personalized, relevant emails based on their needs and desires, they'll either self-solicit, request a meeting, or happily agree to one when you call at precisely the right time.

Technology is the secret sauce that will help you to be exponentially more efficient, effective, and happy. With technology, you can play to your strengths all the time and let automation do the rest.

There are eight components of this innovative fundraising methodology:

1. **Accepting the Pareto principle**

   We've called it the 80/20 rule, but it's more like the 90/10 rule when applied to fundraising. The Pareto principle recognizes that 90 percent of your dollars will come from 10 percent of your donors. It applies to legacy gifts, too: 80–90 percent of your legacy gift dollars will come from 10–20 percent of your legacy gift donors.

2. **Understanding why people really give**

People give because it makes them *feel good*. It's simple, but knowing that doesn't make it easier to raise money. It just puts you on the right footing. It steers you toward an attitude of customer service, empathy, facilitation, and concern. Your fundraising efforts, now aimed at those with tremendous capacity thanks to the acceptance of the Pareto principle, will become customer service oriented. People become partners, not targets. They become human beings with feelings, stories, and passions, not ATM machines.

3. **Employing a feedback loop**

Most nonprofits don't listen to their supporters because it's challenging to listen to so many voices. Instead, they just spray messages *at* them. It's mostly one way. But listening is an essential part of any dialogue. You simply can't build trusting, committed relationships without genuine dialogue. You can't raise money without trusting, committed relationships. Therefore, listening must become an enormous part of your communication strategy.

How can you listen to hundreds, thousands, or millions of supporter voices? It's only possible if you employ technologies to capture your supporters' "verbatims" (self-reported information) and digital body language (online engagement including clicks, views, downloads, time online, recency of online visits, how frequently they engage online, how much time they spend on your site, and so on). These tools help fundraisers cut costs, optimize what they do, and raise gifts efficiently.

4. **Making valuable engagement offers**

Once you accept the Pareto principle, understand why people give, and begin to employ a feedback loop, you'll need to draw people into your marketing funnel. This is where it gets fun and interesting because the employment of valuable engagement offers frees you from interruptive, off-putting, spray-and-pray fundraising outreach efforts. Instead, offers provide an opportunity for you to *give* to your donors—rather than asking them to give to you.

The law of reciprocity states that you're more likely to receive if you give first. It's been proven that the person who gives first usually receives a gift in return from the original recipient that far exceeds the value of the first person's gift (by exponential measures).

Providing valuable engagement offers shows your supporters you care about them. In fact, you can tie together the first three components above with this one to provide your high-capacity supporters an opportunity to fill out a donor survey so they can express why they care, how they want to give, and when. Doing so will make them feel good. MarketSmart has sent out millions of donor surveys on behalf of our clients, and their supporters show their appreciation by giving more. A lot more!

Interestingly, in donor surveys we even ask our clients' supporters if they have donor-advised funds and if they'd consider making ("recommending") a donation with theirs. On the thank you page after the survey, only the respondents who said "yes" to that question get an opportunity to do just that. And they do, with an average donation of over $4,000!

There are other kinds of engagement offers that'll draw your supporters closer to your mission. For some charities, the best ones might be webinars, free content, checklists, and so on. The bottom line is that your offers shouldn't always involve an ask for your supporters and prospects to give you money. That drives them crazy. Mostly, your offers should engage your major and legacy gift donors and supporters in ways that make them feel good. Thanks to the law of reciprocity, they'll return the favor by exponential amounts.

5. **Focusing on lead generation**
Once you've developed your offers aimed at high-capacity donors and buttressed them with a feedback loop that makes the donors feel good, you'll

want to generate leads. In other words, you'll want to present the offers to your list in a way that helps you qualify people who are likely to make major and/or legacy gifts and want to build a relationship and involve themselves more deeply with you and your organization's mission.

At this stage, it's important to recognize that the most vital part of any lead generation effort is your approach. Your outreach must be polite and considerate. Always ask for permission to communicate with your constituents. Ask them to opt in and make it easy for them to opt out. Make sure your efforts are highly contextual, highly personalized, and highly relevant.

Stop spraying and praying. It's disrespectful. Gaining permission is fair; it invites collaboration and builds trust. You should only want people in your funnel because they want to be there. Forcing them to be there will never result in more donations. You can't wash money out of your supporters' bank accounts with a hose! Again, stop spraying and praying!

Present your valuable engagement offers to the right people at the right times. Let them lean in. Make it easy for them to accept your offers and raise their hands, showing interest. Then capture the information they provide about their wants, needs, and desires using landing pages (online forms) and tracking tools that gather their verbatims and digital body language.

6. **Following through with cultivation**
Generating leads is almost a complete waste of time and resources if you don't have a plan to cultivate them. Most leads won't want to take action right away. Proper cultivation encourages people (at this point, your qualified leads) to engage further. Cultivation gives you a chance to "show 'em that you know 'em," that you listened, that you care about their needs, and that they're important to you. Everyone on earth wants to feel important and feel good. Deliberate, meaningful cultivation "drips" are where the magic really happens—as long as they're persistent yet polite, personalized, and relevant. The problem for most fundraisers is that cultivation is overwhelming,

tedious, and time-consuming. You and your staff are already overworked, your data warehouses are a mess, and your staff keeps leaving or changing positions. You know this step is essential, but how on earth can you get it done and get it done right?

Mechanized automation is the most cost-efficient way to provide proper cultivation that builds trust and earns respect. And, thanks to technology, now you can "drip" the right messages to the right people at the right times. If you're not employing these technologies (especially with email drips), you're missing the "yeast that will make the bread rise."

7. **Using a dashboard**

You may be wondering how you can possibly capture all this data and prioritize whom to call (and when). You'll need a dashboard that helps you see your funnel so you can take action. A well-designed dashboard is the glue that ties it all together. It provides clarity, it serves up leads, and it helps you see who's ready for personal outreach. Plus, if it's built right, it should show your leadership and board what kind of revenue could be expected, from whom, and when.

8. **Creating conversions**

Most of your supporters care and want to give. They usually aren't ready to make a decision when you want them to do so, however, because too often you might be guessing when to make your ask.

Conversion efforts are really facilitation efforts. They are the asks. Engagement fundraisers know that if a supporter has qualified herself, informed herself, and involved herself, she'll probably be ready to solicit herself, too. Or, she might be ready for your outreach and even your solicitation.

With these eight core components in place, the guesswork is gone. You'll finally know when to reach out, when to ask, and why. Marrying crucial pieces of information with your supporters' sense of trust and desire for reciprocation (that each donor will have if they're cultivated properly) makes serious magic happen. All of the pieces come together almost effortlessly, and you'll be there to answer their questions and facilitate the closing of the gifts.

The world needs fundraisers like you to enable giving. Your efforts seal the deal. You are the tip of the spear, the boots on the ground. Whiz-bang, strategic, innovative technologies can't work without *you*.

# The VIP Treatment

When you follow the eight components of Engagement Fundraising, you become fanatically focused on making your donors feel good. Major donors may be giving anywhere from $1,000 to $100,000 or more. Legacy donors might take their children's names out of their will and replace them with your charity. Don't these supporters deserve the VIP treatment?

I know it isn't easy. Premium service that results in donor delight is hard to deliver. It takes time, it requires effort, and it involves strategic thinking. I recommend you take a lesson from Ritz-Carlton, the luxury hotel chain that's world renowned for its high level of customer service. Their philosophy on the subject has been well studied and dissected over the years. Here's how they do it:

- Everything they do is focused on genuine care and concern for their customers. Their motto states, "We are ladies and gentlemen serving ladies and gentlemen." Keep in mind that most nonprofits don't even include donors in their mission statements. Shouldn't they be part of that?

- Strategically speaking, they recognize that the lifetime value of a Ritz-Carlton customer is about $250,000. Is that about the same as the lifetime value of your typical major donor (including their legacy gift)?

- Ensuring customer delight is of utmost importance, above all else. In fact, they empower their employees to do whatever it takes to make sure their customers are happy. Based on their analyses, they decided that each employee would be free to spend up to $2,000 to solve a customer problem, per incident, without asking a manager for permission.

- They aim to "wow" their customers so they'll tell their "wow stories" to their friends. Every employee in every department at every Ritz-Carlton gets together for 15-minute meetings to share wow stories with one another regularly. This serves to reinforce their values while maintaining high expectations for themselves across the board.

Ritz-Carlton publishes their Gold Standards on their main website (http:// www.ritzcarlton.com/en/about/gold-standards), making it easy to see what they expect of their staff and what you can expect of them, too:

Three Steps of Service

1. A warm and sincere greeting.

2. Use the guest's name. Anticipation and fulfillment of each guest's needs.

3. Fond farewell. Give a warm good-bye and use the guest's name.

Service Values: I Am Proud to Be Ritz-Carlton

- I build strong relationships and create Ritz-Carlton guests for life.

- I am always responsive to the expressed and unexpressed wishes and needs of our guests.

- I am empowered to create unique, memorable, and personal experiences for our guests.

- I understand my role in achieving the Key Success Factors, embracing Community Footprints, and creating The Ritz-Carlton Mystique.

- I continuously seek opportunities to innovate and improve The Ritz-Carlton experience.

- I own and immediately resolve guest problems.

- I create a work environment of teamwork and lateral service so that the needs of our guests and each other are met.

- I have the opportunity to continuously learn and grow.

- I am involved in the planning of the work that affects me.

- I am proud of my professional appearance, language, and behavior.

- I protect the privacy and security of our guests, my fellow employees, and the company's confidential information and assets.

- I am responsible for uncompromising levels of cleanliness and creating a safe and accident-free environment.[12]

Your high-value donors deserve the same level of service. They want to be heroes in their own minds. They want to find meaning in their lives. They want to feel good. You are their steward and sidekick! You need to support their efforts. You need to partner with them and support them to achieve their goals. Your service needs to make them say, "Wow." You need to deliver consistent, legendary VIP treatment.

Are you now feeling distraught? Don't worry. A lot of the heavy lifting in the 21st century can be accomplished with technology. Many of your supporters, especially legacy donors, might prefer an arm's-length relationship most of the time anyway. So, roll out the red carpet and let them know you care about them more than the other charities that might be vying for their dollars.

---

12 "Gold Standards," The Ritz-Carlton, accessed December 2, 2017, http://www.ritzcarlton.com/en/about/gold-standards.

Give your supporters the VIP treatment. Tell them how awesome they are. Help them learn how to become philanthropists. Give them premium opportunities to involve themselves with your mission. Send them notes and updates. Introduce them to other like-minded individuals. Constantly listen for feedback. Be patient. Be persistent. Be service-oriented. Deliver donor delight!

# The Insider Bulletin

Everyone likes to think of themselves as an insider, right? At MarketSmart, we recognize this and suggest that major donors get a special addition to the regular newsletter that all donors receive. This insider bulletin is not as polished as the mass-produced newsletter. It looks like it was created by you and printed in-house using a desktop printer. The uglier the better as long as it's clear, genuine, and personal with an underground, insider vibe. The stories are real, heartwarming, and timely. They make the donor feel special—like a hero.

The insider bulletin is not a brag sheet. It's not meant to be an opportunity for you to tell your donors how great you are; rather, it's meant to be an opportunity for them to relish how great *they* are. It's intended to remind them that their donations made impact possible, not you and your program staff.

Most importantly, the insider bulletin answers each donor's three most unending questions:

- "What are they doing with my money?"

- "Would my hard-earned dollars yield more impact with another fundraiser at another organization?"

- "How do they make me feel? Good or bad?"

# The Insider Microsite

A variation of the insider bulletin is the insider microsite. It's an online space specially designed for high-capacity VIPs, legacy donors, or people considering becoming one or both. It's a way to answer the three unending questions listed above, as well as inspire them to volunteer, get involved, or refer others to join your shared cause. The insider microsite focuses on how the VIP can leave a legacy, share stories, complete a survey, receive guides to giving, or read a blog created with them in mind. It's engagement that seeks to build community using a channel that's always conveniently available.

Most nonprofits have very narcissistic websites that promote how great they are and how well suited they are to accomplish their mission. It's true that donors need to have belief and confidence in your organization to help them achieve their philanthropic outcomes. But VIPs don't want to be beleaguered with how great you and your organization are. They want to know how great *they* are and how great *they* can be.

An insider microsite is designed with *them* in mind. It shows them how to become philanthropists or legacy society members. It shows them what your organization is doing with their money on their behalf. It proves to them that there's no better place for their hard-earned cash than with you and your organization. And, above all else, it makes them feel good. It helps them feel like the hero in their own life story. It helps them find meaning in their life. It supports their quest for information as they seek support and move themselves through the consideration process. It allows them to recommend donations instantly from their donor-advised funds. It enables them to forward specially written bequest language to their advisors for their estate plans. It helps them explore creative ways to make an impact.

Your main website probably doesn't do all that. And if it does, it's probably buried several clicks away. That's why your VIPs deserve an insider microsite. Unfortunately, your in-house team may not have the time or know-how to provide one. They're usually focused on populist fundraising efforts aimed at low-dollar acquisition, events, or bragging about how great your organization is. That's why you might want to give them this book!

# The Virtual Advisory Board

Another involvement experience for your VIPs is called the Virtual Advisory Board. It takes the microsite idea to a more interactive level. It gives a nonprofit the ability to engage donors wherever they're located through webinar events and virtual meetings. For example, if you funded a campaign that brings fresh water to a village in Africa, what would it mean to you if you could be there virtually as the well is dug? How amazing would it be to tune in weekly to view the progress and be able to ask questions of the staff in real time?

The Virtual Advisory Board is one more way to create two-way communication with your donors. It includes tools to collect donor verbatims and technologies to collect digital body language. Plus, it makes supporters feel like VIPs!

# Staffing Your Fundraising Shop for the 21st Century

Most fundraising teams are highly inefficient because they require people to take on multiple roles. For example, in addition to attending internal meetings, a fundraiser might be analyzing lists, cold-calling, setting appointments, and meeting with donors. There's no way one person can fulfill all of those roles and do them all well. As you start to generate more qualified leads with Engagement Fundraising, it makes more sense than ever to pay attention to the structure of your organization.

The bottom line is that the roles necessary for success should never be combined. Putting people into specializations is the key to exponential gains and tremendous effectiveness.

The division of labor innovation is one of the hallmarks of capitalism. It was first described by Adam Smith in 1776 in his book *The Wealth of Nations*. Later Henry Ford masterfully perfected it in 1908 with the mass production of the Model T. Today, sales teams in the private sector are specializing more than ever.

Here's how it looks:

- Sales manager—oversees operations by supporting staff and coaching everyone to achieve results.

- Marketing—builds awareness, attracts attention, generates interest, and grows desire, plus produces highly qualified leads and cultivates them over time (they call it lead nurturing, not cultivation).

- Outbound outreach—taps into the pipeline of highly qualified leads and further qualifies them before arranging calls or meetings with sales staff.

- Sales—builds relationships based on trust, presents opportunities that align with a prospect's interests, needs, and desires to solve their problems, writes proposals, answers questions, and closes deals.

- Customer success—provides high-level service post-sale to ensure retention, uncover up-sell opportunities, and gain referrals while also acting as the service person, problem solver, and "voice of the customer."

Some of the metrics used by the private sector to keep tabs on results and manage the process include:

- Total team quota ($)

- Average deal size ($)

- Win rate (% of proposals that close)

- Sales cycle (time from opportunity created to closed/won)

- Lifetime value of a customer ($)

- % of deals sourced by marketing

- % of deals sourced by other channels such as referrals

- Number of deals required to achieve team goal

- Number of opportunities required to achieve team goal

- Number of leads required to achieve team goal

Nonprofits would do well to borrow from parts of this private-sector approach in order to "manufacture" exponentially greater results at a high level of efficiency. Instead of asking directors to do everything for their portfolio, nonprofits would benefit from a sales and service structure (described below) with accountability metrics that have been proven effective. They could also increase results by employing a "sales" manager or a part-time coach. Veritus Group, led by Richard Perry and Jeff Schreifels, performs this function for many of the most successful nonprofits in the U.S.

Nonprofits can grow revenues and provide exceptional service for VIPs using the following organizational structure with Outreach Associates, Stewardship Associates, and Gift Officers. The key is understanding the roles so the right people are doing what they do best in a streamlined, scalable fashion.

# Lead Outreach Associates

The job of the Lead Outreach Associate (LOA) is setting up calls or meetings for the Major or Legacy Gift Officer. This is the sole focus of the LOA so this position can potentially be outsourced to telemarketers.

Major and Legacy Gift Officers usually don't like to make cold or warm calls because they're specialists. Their distaste for the activity ensures they'll never be good at outbound calling and emailing, so nonprofits need to let passionate, tenacious Outreach Associates send emails to the qualified leads and handle the cold-calling. They must be experts at engaging with donors contextually and at the right times, using the information gleaned from the dashboard that prioritizes leads based on engagement and likelihood to accept outreach.

The best Lead Outreach Associate is an amiable and friendly people person who is happy to do what skilled Major and Legacy Gift Officers might be less interested in doing, such as:

- Calling, emailing, and connecting on LinkedIn or other social media

- Further qualifying the leads

- Setting appointments

## Stewardship Outreach Associates

In the private sector, the low-hanging fruit can be found in ensuring customer success. The best place to get more revenue and referrals is always from current customers. For nonprofits, the biggest gains can happen fastest if Stewardship Outreach Associates (SOAs) are trained to deliver exceptional service to major and legacy donors. Of course they should answer questions as they're asked, but they should also deliver tremendous value, anticipate needs, and make donors feel exceptionally good.

When it comes to legacy gifts (assuming you've been using the ideas described in this book), your organization might have hundreds or thousands of people in your legacy society. Stewardship Outreach Associates will need to prioritize them by identifying the wealthiest, because, as we've discussed, at least 80 percent of the dollars of any legacy giving program usually comes from less than

20 percent of the donors. Working a strategic stewardship plan will ensure that gifts that have been disclosed, especially the biggest ones, turn into realized dollars.

Stewardship Outreach Associates should be on the lookout for second and third legacy gift opportunities so they get uncovered, cultivated, and closed. For major gifts, the keys involve growing retention rates, increasing donor lifetime value, and inspiring referrals while also generating interest in legacy giving.

SOAs must also be experts at engaging with donors contextually and at the right times thanks to the information gleaned from the dashboard. The best person for this job will also be friendly and ready to enhance the major giving and legacy society experience.

# Major Gift Officer and Legacy Gift Officer

The person holding either of these positions must be amazing at taking opportunities (appointments set up by the LOAs and SOAs) and turning them into big bucks. The Major Gift Officer must be able to link programs and giving opportunities with interests, while the Legacy Gift Officer must have technical estate planning knowledge in order to help donors make bigger gifts. Of course, both need to have exceptional relationship and trust-building skills.

Don't let your Major and Legacy Gift Officers do things they aren't good at doing. They should be booked solid with calls and face-to-face meetings every day, and they should work with a coach (sales manager), even if it's outsourced, to help them manage their funnel, stay focused, and close gifts.

**How to staff your fundraising shop for the 21st century.**

# Building an Outreach-Ready Caseload

Ok. Now you have the right people in the right positions, or perhaps you're all alone. Either way, hopefully you've selected which valuable offers you'll use to generate leads to fill up your pipeline. Remember that a donor survey will probably garner the best results. When you use a survey properly, most of your leads will self-identify their consideration stage, how they rank your organization compared to their other charities, and how important your mission is to them. Once they do that, you'll see that the majority will assign themselves to the awareness or interest stages of the consideration process.

Since most of your leads won't be ready for one-to-one outreach, you should have developed an automated cultivation system. Your cultivation will help them move themselves into the desire stage. Some will even self-solicit.

Now that you've build your system, your supporters will categorize themselves accordingly:

- **Identified supporters** – These folks have not yet leaned in. They are not leads and most certainly are not ready for outreach. They may meet certain requirements according to basic participation and giving metrics (or wealth screening and predictive modeling), but they are not yet ready to be on a gift officer's caseload. Therefore, you should try to help them self-qualify by providing opportunities to take a survey or engage with another qualification offer. Too many organizations identify donor prospects and hand the list to their gift officers without any qualification. This is a huge mistake because it drives gift officers to spend inordinate amounts of time connecting with donors only to find that many are not qualified. That, in turn, leads to frustration among staff, costs the organization money (time = money), and potentially annoys constituents. Your identified supporter list is a good starting point for qualification. It shouldn't be used as the end.

- **Qualified supporters** – Qualified supporters have leaned in. They might have taken a survey, spoken to you on the phone, or met with you face-to-face. Either way, they've answered questions. You know why they care, their interests, passions, consideration stage, and more, including whether or not they have children, would like to give appreciated assets, are interested in supporting your capital campaign, and so on. You can use this information to rank their potential willingness to consider giving at a high level and their likelihood to want to build a deeper relationship with you. Remember, just because a person is wealthy and has given before doesn't necessarily mean they want to be on your caseload. Wealth doesn't make them qualified. Once a wealthy supporter answers some discovery questions, they may reveal that they don't care about your charity as much as the others they support. Don't fret. Remind yourself that the qualification process is designed to help you prioritize your list. The goal is efficiency. Disqualification information helps you stay focused. It saves you time and energy (which saves your organization money). It helps you concentrate on others who might welcome your partnership. Don't be afraid to throw a few fish back in the water.

- **Qualified supporters in cultivation** – Once you have qualified and prioritized your supporters, you can begin to cultivate relationships with them. As a result of your qualification efforts, some will require immediate outreach—hot leads. For instance, a supporter might have responded to a survey stating that she is interested in supporting a particular initiative, has no children, is 82 years old, and has appreciated assets she'd like to give. However, most leads will be warm and qualified for cultivation, not hot. Now that they've self-qualified, it's important to let them self-navigate the stages of the relationship. Leverage technology with this group to cost-effectively deliver highly relevant, personalized email "touches" that never ask for money but provide value and deliver meaningful content politely and persistently over time. This will build their trust and help you further qualify them for your portfolio and outreach as they engage over time. Don't call all of your qualified supporters expecting them to jump at the chance to meet with you. If you have the staff and time available to do that, start by thanking them for taking the survey. Then ask more questions to learn about them. Remember, they leaned in so they'll be more likely to take your call than identified supporters, but they might not be as highly qualified as "outreach-ready" supporters.

- **Highly qualified "outreach-ready" supporters** – As your supporters' trust and desire grow over time thanks to your high-value, highly-personalized, meaningful, and highly relevant cultivation, they'll eventually become *ready* for you to reach out to them. Interestingly, we have found that recency of engagement is the single best indicator that a donor will accept your call—not their wealth or giving history or even their answers to questions (unless one of those answers implies that you should call right away). Recent engagement (most likely done online) proves that your organization is close to the top of their mind. Imagine a qualified supporter in cultivation opens your automated email and clicks on the link to view a video. They watch the entire tear-jerking five-minute story about a beneficiary helped by one of your organization's programs, a program they supported in the past. Don't you think they will be exponentially more likely to *accept* your outreach, meet with you, and give again? Your outreach to those who have engaged deeply won't be cold. It will be warm. In fact, it may even be hot. Some of your "outreach-ready supporters" might even thank you for your attentiveness, concern, and timeliness. This *is* the Disney Experience. Why not give it to them?

- **Caseload supporters** – These are the people you have learned can make an impact and want to connect with your organization on a deeper level. They want to build a relationship with its mission so they can find meaning in their lives. They also want *you* to facilitate the connection so they can get the value they want from their giving. They want to work with you to make an impact. They could become "mega-donors" and a small handful might even develop into truly transformational givers, serious philanthropists giving multi-million dollar donations! These are the folks you want on your caseload. But make no mistake, they don't just appear out of the blue. The best caseloads are built and refined, and the best fundraisers are artisans who assemble them. Moreover, you should understand that caseload supporters can go quiet for a period of time. That's why it's important to monitor their engagement, mostly their digital body language, so you can determine when they become "outreach-ready" once again.

## How Many in Each Category?

If you aim to build a caseload for each gift officer filled with qualified and prioritized "outreach-ready" supporters—wealthy, passionate, donor prospects interested in building a relationship with you so they get value for themselves out of making impactful gifts—at some point you may ask yourself, "How many is the right amount for each category?" There's no perfect answer to this question. Every organization, team, and individual fundraiser is different. Some in the field would prefer to develop unbelievably deep relationships with just 25 highly-qualified, super-wealthy, uber-passionate, and intensely-involved major or principle donors. Others might think that's way too few because losing just one of them could lead to a devastating drop in revenue.

It's widely accepted that the size of the average caseload should be around 150. This size makes a lot of sense in light of research conducted by British anthropologist Robin Dunbar, professor of Experimental Psychology at the University of Oxford. In 1992, Dunbar attracted worldwide attention with his studies related to the cognitive limit of the number of people with whom each of us can maintain stable social relationships. These are relationships in which we know each person well. Dunbar found that there was a correlation between primate brain size in relation to its neocortex and average social group size. For humans, the number of relationships we can maintain was found to be 150. That figure soon became known as Dunbar's Number.

Just because Dunbar's Number makes logical sense, it doesn't necessarily mean 150 is the right size for your own caseload. If you have other duties besides raising money, your caseload should definitely be much smaller, proportionate to your limited bandwidth.

Instead of clinging to widely accepted orthodoxies or Dunbar's research, I recommend you think about it this way: Your job is to raise money, not to make friends. This is a business! Relationships are obviously important. In fact, they are essential. But you owe it to the donors who pay your salary to stay focused on building relationships with people who are likely to make a tremendous impact. Spending exorbitant amounts of time building deep relationships with the wrong people is foolish, and you owe it to the rest of your supporters, the beneficiaries of their donations, your co-workers, and leadership to optimize your caseload as you determine who resides in the categories outlined above:

- Identified supporters

- Qualified supporters

- Qualified supporters in cultivation

- Highly-qualified "outreach-ready" supporters

- Caseload supporters

After careful strategic contemplation, you may be comfortable with having 10,000 identified supporters, 2,000 qualified supporters, 1,800 qualified supporters in cultivation, 20 highly-qualified "outreach-ready" supporters, and 150 caseload supporters. Or, your funnel might be much different especially since your supporters ultimately control the outcome.

| Identified supporters | 10,000 | Have not yet leaned in |
|---|---|---|
| Qualified supporters | 2,000 | Leaned in |
| Qualified supporters in cultivation | 1,800 | Leaned in and worthy of VIP cultivation |
| Highly qualified "outreach-ready" supporters | 20 | Ready for direct one-to-one contact |
| Caseload supporters | 150 | Qualified, prioritized and optimized list of donors |

No matter what you decide, you should constantly evaluate who on your caseload is *un*likely to ever make an impactful gift (or seriously consider one), no matter how wealthy they are, and remove them. You only have so much time in your day. If they do not accept your outreach after a reasonable amount of effort and you cannot build a one-to-one relationship with them, you must let them go! Don't hold on too tightly. Letting go isn't really about giving up. It's about being smart! You'll always have more opportunities waiting in the wings (qualified supporters in cultivation) if you are constantly using an Engagement Fundraising system to generate more leads. Refreshing your caseload is a necessary optimization activity for efficiency and effectiveness.

# Reaching Out

Now that you know who falls into each category, and you've zeroed-in on your highly qualified "outreach-ready" supporters, it's finally time to contact them. Generating, capturing, and prioritizing leads is fun, but if you want to someday get to the solicitation step, you have to reach out and set an appointment.

For most, getting the meeting is the hardest part of the job. Remember, as Jerold Panas pointed out in *Mega Gifts*, "It is harder to get an appointment than to secure the gift." He continued by saying, "Getting the appointment is 85 percent of getting the gift."

Although you have qualified your leads, cultivated them, and determined who is ready for your outreach, it's likely that the donor still might not trust you. They may have belief and confidence in your organization and its mission, but *you* are a different story. You are unfamiliar, and all of us have been taught to keep away from strangers. Not to mention, unfortunately, they've probably been interrupted or harassed by other poorly trained fundraisers in the past who failed to provide value to them.

## The Valley of Distrust

Simply stated, although your highly qualified supporters might appear to be outreach-ready, they don't know and trust *you* yet. Consequently, the first 20 seconds of your initial contact will probably be a bit awkward and uncomfortable for both of you. Make no mistake, it's your responsibility to find a way to bridge this valley of distrust. It's up to you to cross the chasm.

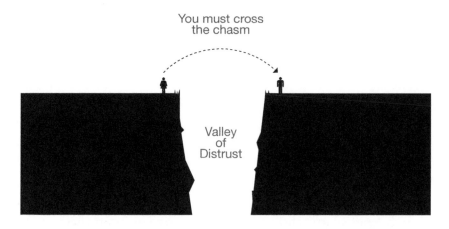

I came to this realization as a result of my own ineffectual experience with outbound telemarketing at MarketSmart. In order to set appointments to demonstrate our products and services, we were cold-calling and interrupting qualified prospects (fundraisers like you, not donors) who engaged with our content recently online. Not surprisingly, we were met with resistance and hang-ups.

Looking back now, it makes a lot of sense. We had gotten off-track and our cold-callers embraced a "taking" philosophy instead of focusing on giving. Everyone knows you have to give to get. For some strange reason, I had forgotten this cardinal rule. I'd become self-centered because I wanted those appointments.

To make matters worse, I gave the cold-callers a goal of setting two appointments per day. They were pushed to reach a quantitative goal which they pursued with no regard for the other person on the phone. We were doing the very things I preach against—interrupting and annoying the people we wanted to help. For that, I sincerely apologize. We failed.

Then, we pivoted.

As more and more prospects unsubscribed from my blog and asked to be removed from our list, the truth hit me like a bag of rocks. You can't build a relationship without trust, and an exchange of money will only happen when a proper exchange of value exists. So, we went back to practicing what we preach. We turned things around by developing an outreach methodology that we named *engagement calling*. Today, I'm convinced that it is the most effective way to cross the chasm over the valley of distrust.

# Never Cold Call Again

Our engagement calling methodology also works for fundraisers because it bridges the gap between marketing communications (lead generation or cultivation) and appointment setting calls. If you have staffed your shop for the 21st century with Lead Outreach Associates, I suggest you train them on engagement calling to ensure that they understand how to advance the relationship so the donor will become exponentially more willing to accept your next call, and the next, and even your request for a face-to-face meeting. Here's how it works.

Engagement calling is a mandatory two-step process at a minimum. Restraint is key. The goal is not to set an appointment. Instead, it's to find a way to *give* to your supporter before you ask to receive anything from them, including a meeting. While it can be arduous and time-consuming, the effort is unquestionably justifiable because of its mutual benefit to you and your donor. It will help you cross the chasm over the valley of distrust while helping your donor grow comfortable with you. Although you might feel like you aren't accomplishing much at first, realize that patience is actually a tremendously worthwhile form of action. Aristotle once said, "Patience is bitter but its fruit is sweet."

# Call One – Use Reciprocity and Discovery to Build Rapport and Trust

In order to remedy the bad reputation most donors ascribe to poorly trained fundraisers, the first call must employ the law of reciprocity entwined with a discovery exercise to build rapport and trust. Once you connect with your supporter, you must provide value immediately, in the first five to 20 seconds of the call to avoid a polite disconnection or immediate dial tone. Try this:

- Project confidence and enthusiasm. Attitude is 80 percent of the battle and people can sense yours even on the telephone.

- Speak clearly and succinctly. Many of your supporters may be older and hard of hearing. Plus, you only have five to 20 seconds!

- Be direct. Introduce yourself and immediately put them at ease by saying, "Hi _____. This is _____calling from _____. I'm not calling to ask for a donation."

- Without delay, go right into the reason for your call (to add value) by saying, "I'm calling from the donor engagement team. My job is to reach out to special supporters like you to say 'thank you,' and find out *how we can give you what you need to make sure you feel good about your investment in our charity.*" Do not say, "How are you doing?" It's a waste of time and the person on the other end of the line will view it as insincere. Remember, you are only calling to *give* to her.

- Next, without pausing or taking a breath, start asking questions by saying, "But first, I was wondering what inspired your gift of $_____ on _____, 2018." Or you might ask, "Why do you care about our mission?" Or, better yet, point out that you received her survey and then ask her a very personalized and relevant question that relates to the information she previously provided. The important thing to note is that you must go into the discovery exercise right after you employed the law of reciprocity and your donor realizes that it's in their best interest to stay on the line with you.

Make sure the call is all about *them*, not about you or your employer. Your donor doesn't want to hear how great your organization is or what your CEO wants. They don't want to hear that you aim to show them or tell them about this or that. No! They want to tell you why they care. They want to convey *their* story and *their* needs. They want to hear how great *they* are, how *they* can be the hero in *their* own life story, and how *they* can realize the best version of themselves. Let them!

Again, thank them and show them your immediate goal is to give to them. Prove that you are calling merely to deliver value by providing deeper engagement opportunities, information, and involvement offers. Explain that you are their conduit. You help generous, caring people like them understand what your organization did (and will do) with their money. And, you are calling to help them see how amazing *they* are for caring about the organization's mission.

Throughout the call, make sure you project a spirit of service and partnership. Operate as a facilitator and problem solver as you ask poignant questions about your supporter's needs. Then, listen. Use your questions to probe gently and uncover interests, passions, and desires (reasons why they care). In most cases, this approach will set them at ease instantly and your donor will answer your questions. Finally, ask for permission to follow-up (and prescribe when).

Remember, do *not* ask for an appointment or a donation during this call unless your donor begs to give or insists on a meeting. Otherwise, it is strictly forbidden. While it may be tempting to ask them for money or a meeting since you have them on the line, resist the temptation to do something that is convenient for you and annoying for them. According to Dr. James, "You don't ever want to do something that makes people believe you don't care what they think." If you ask for money or a meeting on your first engagement call, they will feel that you only asked poignant questions about their needs so they would agree to a meeting or give you money, not because you were actually interested in their answers.

Give first. Build trust. Be patient!

## Call Two – Build More Trust, Meet Needs, and Determine Consideration Stage

Let's pretend you work for a hospital foundation. On the agreed upon date, call again.

This time make your introduction with polite pleasantries. Remind your donor who you are and recount part of your previous conversation. For example, "Hi, _____. This is _____ from _____. I called last week to thank you for giving to our hospital. I was so interested in hearing about your husband and how the hospital made a difference to your family during his illness. Again, I'm not calling to ask you for money."

Next, conduct more discovery. Now that you know the donor better, you should think through your questions before you make this call. Write them down and have them in front of you. The point of your engagement call is to further build trust and determine the needs of your potential donor so that you can potentially meet them. Therefore, after you uncover more about why she cares, you'll want to consider asking additional questions to determine where she resides in the consideration process. See if she might accept more offerings, be willing to engage further, or want to explore giving opportunities to see if one could be a good fit.

For instance, try it this way:

- encourage her to expand on statements made previously;

- then, to determine her consideration stage, you either:

  (1) suggest more valuable content at a low level, perhaps sharing a report or a video of children enjoying the new pediatric wing of the hospital;

  (2) provide opportunities for deeper involvement that are not gift-oriented, perhaps taking a tour of the hospital; or

  (3) offer a chance to engage face-to-face with you to evaluate fit and discuss funding options or ways of making an impact.

Once you know where the donor is on her journey, you can act accordingly to meet her comfort level. It will be easy to recognize when you have provided enough value and built ample trust because the donor will let you know. Then you set the appointment.

Make no mistake, at some point, you have to set the appointment and you have to ask for the donation. Although, with engagement calling, the process will be less distressing for you and your donor. Since you've carefully and strategically generated leads, prioritized your list to reach out to the right people at the right time, and used engagement calling to build trust and serve your donor and your mission in the best possible way, the appointment will almost set itself naturally. Then you'll finally get a chance to do what you do best—build deep relationships with amazing people who can make a consequential impact.

When you use technology to qualify your leads and then cultivate them properly, you'll build deeper, more meaningful relationships with the right people and manage your optimized caseload more intently. Don't worry if the refined numbers might be smaller. It's *not* a numbers game. In fact, it's not a game at all. You are dealing with real people. If you want to be successful, you have to change your mindset from "ask, ask, ask" and "take, take, take" to a donor-centric model of giving.

Don't let your boss, your leadership, or your program directors force you into doing what they perceive as best for them and your organization. Be donor-centric. Provide massive value for the qualified people that matter most, and employ engagement call techniques to cross the chasm of the valley of distrust. Then continue to provide service and value until the time comes for you to offer giving opportunities that match needs.

It's that simple. Be patient. Use reciprocity and discovery to build rapport and trust. Be service oriented and provide value. Then determine the prospect's consideration stage so you can meet their needs. Fundraising isn't about manipulation or coercion. It isn't about taking. It's about giving. Give more to your donors with engagement calling. Then everybody wins.

## Are You Ready to Engage?

By this point, you should have a deep understanding of Engagement Fundraising and its fundamental concepts. You may even be contemplating restructuring your team to be more efficient and effective. But the question remains: Are you ready to engage?

If you agree with me that fundraising is broken, I hope I've also shown you how we can fix it. The solution is here.

Engagement Fundraising is not only fair to you, it's fair to donors. It gives them the respect they deserve. It enables them to move themselves through the consideration continuum at the time of their choosing. They build their own awareness, qualify themselves, inform themselves, and self-solicit. More gifts can be closed at a much faster pace when an organization knows who's most likely to act and can then present prospects with valuable offers matched to where they are in their journey.

When donors feel no pressure to act and are able to give their permission for outreach, engagement is accepted and welcomed. If you want to fix the broken system that fundraising is today, donors need to be at least 50 percent of the equation, not an afterthought. From my perspective as a marketer, as well as my perspective as a ticked-off donor, Engagement Fundraising is the best way to enhance the relationship between fundraisers, charities, and the donors who support them.

It's a win-win-win. Donors are treated better, fundraisers can focus on highly qualified prospects who are ready to act, and charities raise more money for their beneficiaries. The donor gets what they want—to feel good—and the charity spends exponentially less time and money because you aren't required to make it all happen manually.

Engagement Fundraising works because it makes supporter engagement and involvement with an organization's mission (and its beneficiaries) easier, faster, more convenient, more personalized, more relevant, and more fun. The business of fundraising must evolve as a service industry and reflect shifts in how donors behave and how they want to be treated. Embracing, not resisting, changes in communication and technology will reinvigorate the system with happier fundraisers, happier donors, and more money raised to make the world a better place. After all, isn't that why you got into fundraising in the first place?

## Will you become an engagement fundraiser?

For the sake of donors, volunteers, advocates, and members everywhere who want to change the world but need an organization bigger than them to get it done, I hope you'll become an engagement fundraiser.

For the sake of the employees at nonprofits who work tirelessly for the donors, volunteers, advocates, and members, I hope you'll become an engagement fundraiser.

And most of all, for the people who desperately depend on all of the above, I hope you'll become an engagement fundraiser. People like my wife, Nessa, whom I love more than anything else in the world. You can help her and others like her—the sick, the poor, and the hungry. The wounded, underserved, and distressed. The defenseless, needy, and unfortunate.

With Engagement Fundraising, you can help make the world a better place for all of humanity for generations to come.

# Appendix

## Glossary: A New Lexicon for 21st-Century Fundraising

I hope the following explanation of the terms I've used in this book are helpful. Some of them, like *Engagement Fundraising* and *digital donor concierge,* are my own. Some are used in other sectors and I've taken the liberty of using them to reinvent the fundraiser's vocabulary. I hope you'll embrace them as you move forward as a fundraiser dedicated to your cause—and dedicated to the engagement and delight of your donors.

**Actionable Intelligence** – Information that can help you focus your activities and costs on the people who will most likely make the greatest financial impact the soonest; verbatims and digital body language.

**Digital Body Language** – Online engagement behaviors of supporters such as email clicks, page views, time on site, frequency of visits, etc.; what supporters do as opposed to what they say.

**Digital Donor Concierge** – MarketSmart's pioneering technology that uses artificial intelligence and machine learning to provide a VIP experience to donors by delivering perfectly timed offers that are effective and self-actuating.

**Donor Delight** – Best-in-class customer service in the nonprofit sector; aka stewardship or donor relations.

**Donor Journey** – The consideration process of a donor that's viewed as a continuum from awareness to interest, desire, and action, repeat giving and finally legacy giving.

**Engagement Fundraising** – A donor-centric approach to fundraising that focuses on making offers of valuable content to engage supporters and make them feel good until they're ready to make a gift.

**Feedback Loop** – The two-way conversation created when a fundraiser delivers valuable content that causes a supporter to opt in and reciprocate in some way. As the supporter provides additional information, the fundraiser is able to listen and respond in ways that grow the relationship.

**Four Selfs** – The four behaviors that allow donors to navigate the fundraising process on their own: self-qualification, self-education, self-involvement, and self-solicitation.

**Hard Offers** – Offers that ask supporters to take action or make a commitment at the time of the offer. Offers that ask supporters to respond or engage in ways that do not require much significant or careful consideration.

**Marketing Automation** – Technology and software that uses actionable intelligence to automatically deliver highly relevant, personalized, and contextual online experiences that satisfy donor needs with the right information at the right time.

**Progressive Profiling** – Collecting actionable intelligence to monitor supporters and capture new information about them as they move through the donor journey.

**Self-Solicitation** – The act of moving oneself to the point of giving as opposed to being "moved" by a fundraiser.

**Soft Offers** – Offers that ask supporters to respond or engage in ways that do not require much significant or careful consideration.

**Show Up and Throw Up Fundraisers** – Annoying fundraisers that talk about their own agenda instead of listening and paying attention to the wants and needs of the donor.

**Spray and Pray Fundraising** – Aiming direct mail and spam at people who could care less.

**Verbatims** – The exact words used by your prospects and supporters to tell you why they care; what supporters say as opposed to what they do.

CPSIA information can be obtained
at www.ICGtesting.com
Printed in the USA
BVHW03s0439150518
516251BV00002B/40/P

9 781732 262812